STUDIES IN ASIAN AMERICANS
RECONCEPTUALIZING CULTURE, HISTORY, AND POLITICS

Edited by
Franklin Ng
California State University, Fresno

A ROUTLEDGE SERIES

STUDIES IN ASIAN AMERICANS
RECONCEPTUALIZING CULTURE, HISTORY, AND POLITICS
FRANKLIN NG, *General Editor*

POLITICIZING ASIAN AMERICAN LITERATURE
Towards a Critical Multiculturalism

Youngsuk Chae

Routledge
New York & London

First published 2008
by Routledge
270 Madison Ave, New York, NY 10016

Simultaneously published in the UK
by Routledge
2 Park Square, Milton Park, Abingdon, Oxon OX14 4RN

Routledge is an imprint of the Taylor & Francis Group, an informa business

Typeset in Adobe Garamond by IBT Global
Printed and bound in the United States of America on acid-free paper by IBT Global

Library of Congress Cataloging-In-Publication data
Chae, Youngsuk.
  Politicizing Asian American literature : towards a critical multiculturalism / by Youngsuk Chae.
    p. cm. — (Studies in Asian Americans)
  Includes bibliographical references and index.
  ISBN 0-415-96099-1
    1. American literature—Asian American authors—History and criticism. 2. Politics in literature.   3. Multiculturalism in literature.   4. Yamashita, Karen Tei, 1951–Tropic of orange.   5. Ozeki, Ruth L. My year of meats.   6. Emigration and immigration in literature.   7. Asian Americans—Intellectual life.   8. Identity (Psychology) in literature.   9. Asian Americans in literature.   10. Immigrants in literature.   I. Title.

PS153.A84C46 2007
810.9'895—dc22   2007018710

ISBN10: 0-415-96099-1 (hbk)
ISBN10: 0-203-94244-2 (ebk)

ISBN13: 978-0-415-96099-1 (hbk)
ISBN13: 978-0-203-94244-4 (ebk)

To the Memory of My Father

Contents

Preface

Politicizing Asian American Literature examines multiculturalism from the perspective of Asian American writings. This project is my attempt in essence to create a space for a counter-narrative to delineate the ongoing discrimination and exploitation practiced against race, ethnicity, and gender within and outside the United States, and my standing as an outsider within has inspired me to read the dominant American culture and politics with a critical gaze.

In this book, I have made a distinction between politically acquiescent and politically conscious Asian American multicultural writings in order to examine whether racial or ethnic minority writers demonstrate an awareness of unequal power relations along race/ethnicity lines, or whether they allow themselves to be projected as cultural "others," while conforming to existing unequal power relations. My attempt to politicize Asian American literature is purposely framed in order to arouse a critical consciousness among Asian Americans beyond ethnic differences.

One goal of my project is to bring attention to writers who seek to highlight a critical awareness of Asian Americans' social and economic status and their position as "unassimilable aliens," "yellow perils," "coolies," "modern-day high tech coolies," or as a "model minority," notions that have been ideologically woven through the complex interactions of capital and labor in American cultural and labor history.

Most popularly received Asian American writings have in fact been silent about what we might call the material histories that have conditioned the lives of immigrants in the United States. The literary representations produced by Asian American writers have failed to reflect the differentiation practiced towards minority immigrants along race/ethnicity lines. Conversely, a discrete body of politically engaging Asian American multicultural writings has sought to arouse critical awareness of how minority groups have been systematically differentiated according to their race, ethnicity, gender, and nation in the developmental process of U.S. capitalism. In a departure from the celebration of Asian immigrants' success stories, which are mostly silent about the political and economic conditions that have brought people to the United States, I have attempted to reveal with a dissident voice how immigrant labor has been economically and ideologically exploited in the process of U.S. capital formation, and how the issues of U.S.-centered globalization and differentiation of immigrants within the nation are interconnected. In this context, I have recast the phenomenon of Asian migration against the background of U.S. neo-colonialism and global capitalism in order to examine the ambivalent position of Asian immigrants as middlemen in the U.S. economy, to demystify the stereotyped image of Asian Americans as the "model minority," and to challenge the white dominant image of "America" usually underscored in promoting multiculturalism and diversity.

Although the term "Asian American" was first used after the civil rights movement in order for it to be possible to claim a lawful right as representative citizens and reconstruct own "collective identities," articulating the distinction of Asians in America through literary works has been utilized to the point that it fosters an image of Asian Americans as "cultural others." Being Asian American does not mean that one has to dwell on being a racial/ethnic minority. Rather, articulating racial/ethnic distinctions should be an attempt to frame a question concerning the discriminatory policies directed against minorities in society, and what Asian Americans or Asian American writers should do is move beyond the boundaries of ethnic differences and develop a sense of critical consciousness and a strong solidarity among different racial/ethnic groups.

Despite my efforts to shed light on some less acknowledged yet politically conscious Asian American writings, upon finishing this project I find that it is still just a beginning—a supplication for greater attention to literary works about and by the underrepresented groups among the marginalized Asians in the United States. Any remaining limitations, misinterpretations, or errors in this book I lay solely to my own responsibility and account.

Acknowledgments

I am very grateful to have an opportunity to express my gratitude to the many people who have emotionally, intellectually, and financially helped and supported me throughout this long journey. I sincerely want to thank Carla Mulford for her invaluable comments and keen advice on my project as well as her intellectual mentoring, heartwarming encouragement, and continuing support. Her academic professionalism has shown me so many good examples to follow. I am also greatly indebted to Aldon Nielsen. His careful reading of each chapter of this book greatly helped me to rethink of my arguments in more sophisticated ways. Mark Morrisson offered much-appreciated suggestions at the conceptual level of this project. I am grateful for his advice and generous assistance to me. A special debt of gratitude is owed to Reiko Tachibana, who continually offered words of encouragements and helped me broaden my perspective of Asian American literature. My gratitude goes to Jake Jakaitis for his introduction to critical "ethnic" literature at the outset of this project. I am also thankful to Jung-Il Do for teaching me the importance of being a critical scholar.

Colleagues and friends in different locations have encouraged and inspired this work at various points, and I express my respect and thanks to Jung-wan Yu, Myong-ho Lee, Kijung Kwon, Bong-hee Oh, Susan Jakaitis, Shiaw-fen Ferng, Louis and Walter Sommers for their friendship and encouragement over the years. In particular, I would like to thank Donald Jackman for carefully reading my manuscript and helping with proofreading.

I am very grateful to the staff at Routledge who made the publication of this book possible. I especially want to thank Benjamin Holtzman, the research editor of Routledge, for expressing an interest in my book project and for helping me with my manuscript. I also thank Eleanor Chan and Elizabeth Levine for their kind assistance. I am particularly grateful to

Franklin Ng, the editor-in-chief, for giving me incisive and valuable suggestions for the revision of this book, and I owe a great deal to other anonymous editorial board members who provided helpful comments.

Most of all, I am greatly indebted to the loving support of Won-kwon Park and Jung-Ja Lee, and I am thankful to my mother, sisters, and brothers in Korea for their caring and supporting of my scholarly pursuit. Lastly, I reserve my deepest thanks to my daughter, Soobin, for her humor and patience, and my husband, Changjoon, for his intellectual companionship and trust in me even at the most difficult time.

Introduction

"Who Consumes Multiculturalism?"

> Multiculturalism has acquired a quality akin to spectacle. The metaphor that has displaced the melting pot is the salad. A salad consisting of many ingredients is colorful and beautiful, and it is to be consumed by someone. Who consumes multiculturalism is the question begging to be asked.
>
> —Angela Davis

American society was already multicultural long before the term "multiculturalism" emerged in the 1970s. By multiculturalism we mean the acceptance of difference founded in cultural diversity and ethnic values such as language, food, traditions, attitudes or cultural heritages. Unlike the "melting pot" model of cultural blending, which requires racial/ethnic minorities or immigrants to conform to the standard and core values of the society, multiculturalism has given the largest scope to reciprocity with respect to the cultural influences that racial minority or immigrant groups have brought with them to the United States. Although the idea of multiculturalism spread widely in the 1980s through slogans related to cultural pluralism, how the term was first used or developed remains vague, and questions related to political and ideological meanings and implications of the term have been continuously raised.

According to Christopher Newfield and Avery Gordon, the idea of multiculturalism originated at a primary and secondary educational level as part of an attempt to promote a "multidimensional approach relatively foreign to the compartmentalized knowledge of universities, addressing institutional factors along with questions of personal identity, bi-and tricultural relations, community culture, teacher attitudes and behaviors, school administrative structure, and local politics and economics, among others."[1] Multiculturalism, in its original conception, seems to have been perceived in the sense of a reformist movement against assimilation's "melting pot" ideology, which requires racially and culturally diverse groups of people to blend into the dominant culture of the society. Regardless of whether multiculturalism emerged as an opponent of a monolithic culture or as an alternative to white "American" society, debate has continued about whether U.S. multiculturalism dilutes or disguises racial and political consciousness in the era of the post-civil rights movement. This debate currently revolves around whether the multicultural inclusion of difference is a product of the "state-sponsored policy" or whether emphasis on cultural diversity tends to reduce immigrants to essentially different ethnic groups and implicitly fosters "cultural separatism" in the name of difference and cultural pluralism.

U.S. multiculturalism's celebration of cultural diversity and pluralism has been challenged on account of its tendency to shift attention from racial contexts to cultural terrains. Multiculturalism's framework of understanding racially and culturally different groups in cultural contexts has been blamed for its "color blindness" or for blocking racially critical consciousness.[2] For instance, if we understood certain minority groups' poverty in a cultural context, the problem might be attributed to their lack of effort or culturally less motivated attitudes towards education, rather than to the essential structural inequality. In other words, multiculturalism's decontextualizing tendency in interpreting social and racial issues under the rubric of culture has eventually contributed to veiling the existing structure of unequal power in the society. Despite diversity and cultural pluralism becoming to some degree a fact of existence in "American" society, U.S. multiculturalism's emphasis on difference has not been accompanied by a corresponding reality in which the structural problems of racial discrimination and economic inequality are foregrounded or reduced or resolved.

U.S. multiculturalism, in spite of its recognition and appreciation of different cultures, is in my view still premised upon an underlying assumption that perceives racial and cultural minorities as the others, while leaving the color of white ethnic culture invisible in the background, enabling a toning down of racial issues. The politically neutralizing tendency of U.S. multiculturalism suggests indirectly that the acceptance of cultural diversity or pluralism is likely to be tolerated as long as it does not threaten the power structure of the society, and that it may remain permissible within the boundary that white dominant (bourgeois) groups set up.

In spite of the fact that "American" is itself a hyphenated identity, "American" society instead has visualized the color as its distinctive element. Just as the reason many non-whites were brought to the United States is related to maintenance of the political, ideological, and economic system based on labor exploitation through racial stratification, the complex interaction between race and class, which is invisibly working in the United States, has not been weakened—even after the idea of multiculturalism has become prevalent in the society. In this respect, Angela Davis says that multiculturalism in the name of cultural diversity and pluralism has veiled the structural inequality in which racial and ethnic minorities have been situated economically. As Angela Davis has asked,

> What happens when we shift our arguments away from charges of racism and begin to talk about difference, diversity, and multiculturalism? "Difference" and "diversity" are descriptive: people are different; cultures are diverse. In this context, we must be aware of the fact that multiculturalism can easily become a way to guarantee that these differences and diversities are retained superficially while becoming homogenized and harmonized politically, especially along axes of class, gender, and sexuality. Although this is not an inevitability, multiculturalism can become a polite and euphemistic way of affirming persisting, unequal power relationships by representing them as equal differences.[3]

With Davis, I believe that multiculturalism, while celebrating cultural diversity, has lacked critical discussions related to hegemony, racial conflicts, and exploitation of immigrants as cheap labor and has helped to cover over the existing racial conflicts and class issues.

Regardless of its intention, U.S. multiculturalism's emphasis on different cultural values and ethnic diversity has helped to advertise the image of "America" as a place where people can have a freedom to keep their own culture as well as to pursue their dream in the United States. Despite its ideal image, the real life experiences that immigrants or racial minorities have in the United States are still replete with racial discrimination, labor exploitation, and socio-economic marginalization.[4] Moreover, the economic difficulty in which racial minorities are situated has been laid at the feet of individuals' ability and efforts rather than attributing the structure of inequality as the main cause of poverty. By foregrounding differences and diversity without questioning an existing unequal power structure and exploitation of labor against nonwhites, ethnic minorities or immigrants, the practice of multiculturalism in the United States has in effect obscured the interconnected issues of race, gender, and class, and it eventually has contributed towards maintaining the power structure of the U.S. society.

For the second and third generation of Asian immigrants, those who were born in the United States and grew up in the American educational system, acculturation to American society has taken place naturally and rapidly over time. Their desire for establishing an economically and socially stable position cannot be judged simply by saying that they were "Americanized." When we apply the term "multiculturalism" to racial minorities or in this case the second and third generation of Asian immigrants, the important thing that we need to ask, in my view, is whether the social discrimination toward racial minorities and structural inequality of those minorities have been reduced enough for them to appreciate cultural diversity and the "democratic" American society, and whether they have also consciously reacted to unequal power relations and institutionalized racism. Part of the criticisms that current discussion of U.S. multiculturalism has received for its politically neutralizing or disengaging or perhaps conservative attitudes resonates in the manner in which the myth of Asian Americans as a "model minority" is ideologically woven to sustain the system's stability.

In the case of Asian Americans and Asian immigrants, U.S. multiculturalism and its celebration of cultural diversity have aligned with the boosterized image of Asian Americans as a "successful" minority due to their cultural values and ethnic attitudes. The media-fostered image of Asian immigrants as a "model minority" has helped to advertise the myth of "America" as a multicultural "democratic" society" and "land of promise." The publication of writings by Asian immigrants or their descendents under the rubric of multicultural literature or "ethnic literature," to a large extent characterized by "successful" stories, has also contributed towards underrepresentation of the poverty, racial discrimination, social oppression, and economic inequality that most minorities have been suffering.

To my thinking, most "popular" Asian American multicultural writings have not situated their narratives in specific socio-political and historical contexts. Rather, they tend to decontextualize political and economic circumstances and the structural inequality that racial minorities and immigrants have faced by focusing mainly on issues of cultural conflict, generational gaps with their parent generation, or identity crisis. The issue of identity crisis, which has been the most common theme in multicultural literature, is depicted in most "popular" Asian American writings as immigrants' failure to adjust to U.S. culture with respect to language, attitudes, food, and customs. This perspective is not much different from other narratives of U.S. multiculturalism in that they foreground cultural aspects in interpreting the difficulties those minorities have faced. The issue of identity crisis cannot be solely understood in cultural contexts. Rather the identity crisis that minorities have experienced is an ideological product of the socio-political and economic circumstance of the period, as we have seen for example through the cases of Japanese internment after World War II and special registration of non-citizen Arabs after September 11, 2001.

Thus I am seeking to achieve a higher degree of critical consciousness in order to understand how the image of Asian immigrants as a "model minority" was ideologically woven and how the "popular" image pinned on them has been paradoxically working against Asian immigrants while putting them in among whites and blacks, or blacks and Chicanos/Latino Americans.

TOWARD A CRITICAL MULTICULTURALISM

Many writings by immigrants or the descendents of immigrants from Asia have been published in the past several decades, with many books published under the rubric of "ethnic literature" or multicultural literature. However, the term multiculturalism has been contested. For instance, Henry Giroux addresses some of the issues at stake:

> Two issues are often overlooked in current public discussions of mul-
> ticulturalism. On one hand there are the systematic, economic, politi-
> cal, and social conditions that contribute to the domination of many
> subordinate groups. On the other hand, too little attention is paid to
> the sundry struggles subordinate groups undertake through the devel-
> opment of counternarratives that make them the subject rather than the
> object of history.[5]

In a similar vein, E. San Juan Jr., argues, "The Asian American citizen who articulates her subjecthood, her subalternity, through multiculturalism (assimilation via acculturation lurks not far behind) betrays an ignorance of the lopsided distribution of power and wealth in a racially stratified society."[6] What both Giroux and San Juan Jr. criticize is the social condition that American multiculturalism is generating because it passes over the "historical density of collective resistance and revolt" and eventually contributes to the dominant ideology.

However, instead of throwing away the term, which is already part of American reality, I would rather point out how the term has been used or exploited for the sake of U.S. ideological or institutional justification, and then propose an alternative multiculturalism in opposition to the institutionalized version. In order to clarify the different ideological constructions around the meaning of the term, it will be useful to make distinctions among various multiculturalisms. Multiculturalism should not be regarded as a singular term that has a monolithic definition; rather, multiculturalisms—plural—have different standpoints depending on the perspectives of those employing the terms.

Peter McLaren divides the current discussion of multiculturalism into "conservative multiculturalism," "liberal multiculturalism," "left-liberal multiculturalism," and "critical and resistance multiculturalism." According to McLaren, conservative multiculturalism uses the term "diversity" to "cover up the ideology of assimilation" that undergirds its position. In this view, ethnic groups are "reduced to add-ons" to the dominant culture: "Before you can be 'added on' to the dominant United States culture you must first adopt the essentially Euro-American patriarchal norms of the 'host' country."[7] Liberal multiculturalism considers that "equality is absent in United States society, not because of black or Latino cultural deprivation, but because social and educational opportunities do not exist that permit everyone to compete equally in the capitalist marketplace." Left-liberal multiculturalism emphasizes "cultural differences" related to race, class, gender, and sexuality, but McLaren points out that the left-liberal position nevertheless "tends to exoticize 'otherness' in a nativistic retreat that locates difference in a primeval past of cultural authenticity."[8] Critical multiculturalism, which McLaren wants to pursue, interrogates the "construction of difference and identity in relation to a radical politics," and it is positioned "against the neo-imperial romance with monoglot ethnicity grounded in a shared or 'common' experience of 'America' associated with conservative and liberal strands of multiculturalism."[9] In spite of his useful distinctions among various strands of multiculturalisms, I sense the necessity to attempt the use of a critical set of terms to distinguish among different kinds of multiculturalisms, especially in the light of the case presented by Asian American literature.

Thus, in my discussion of multiculturalism in the light of Asian American writings, I will draw a contrast between politically acquiescent multiculturalism and politically conscious multiculturalism. Although this binary of polarized contrasts might fall into the danger of over-simplification, my establishment of a set of terms particular to the writings of and about Asian Americans is symbolically drawn in order to bring a critical awareness of their social and economic status and their position as "unassimilable aliens," "yellow perils," "coolies," "modern-day high tech coolies," or as a "model minority," notions that were ideologically woven through the complex interactions of capital and labor in U.S. labor history.

To my thinking, it is possible to identify politically acquiescent multiculturalism as conservative—whether assimilation is forced or not—with regard to the socioeconomic and political conditions that have displaced people from their countries of origin, with regard to racial discrimination, and with regard to economic inequality in the United States. Most "popular" ethnic or conservative multicultural writings tend not to address the contradictory rhetoric that the U.S. government has taken toward immigrants throughout its history. By failing to ground their narratives in specific historical and political contexts while celebrating their assimilating success story, politically acquiescent multicultural writings, in this respect, serve to sustain the U.S. power structure. What politically acquiescent multiculturalists reflect through their writings is the narrative of a "model minority," a status "honorably" given by the U.S. for the price of an obedient silence.

Politically acquiescent Asian American multicultural writings correspond to the institutionalized U.S. multiculturalism, because both celebrate cultural diversity while masking unequal power structures and exploitation of labor against racial minorities and because they both in some ways "commodify" cultural differences as well as reinforce the stereotype of Asian Americans as a "model minority." In my view, institutionalized U.S. multiculturalism and politically acquiescent Asian American multicultural writings have helped to promote the common image of "America" as a "land of opportunity" and have played a role as a puppet advertising the myth of "America" as real.

By contrast, politically conscious Asian American multicultural works delineate a critical distance from white middle-class dominant "American" culture and politics. Whereas politically acquiescent Asian American multicultural writings are mostly silent about labor exploitation toward racial minorities as well as the unequal economic structure faced by Asian Americans, politically conscious Asian American multicultural writings situate their stories in specific historical, political, economical, and legal contexts and draw our attention to the circumstances that have conditioned the lives of Asian immigrants. Politically conscious Asian American writings, which I regard as a critical multiculturalism, focus on depicting Asian immigrants whose lives have been determined by the historical or economic conditions (i.e., the development of U.S. capitalism and the ongoing U.S.-centered global restructuring of capitalism) as well as restrictive immigration policies. What politically conscious Asian American multicultural writings convey is an expression of disagreement with the U.S. political and economic policy toward other worlds as well as a reaction against the United States' inconsistent and ambivalent attitudes and policies affecting minorities and immigrants within the nation.

It is part of my intention to broaden the spectrum of institutionalized U.S. multiculturalism beyond its focus on "cultural diversity" and "ethnic difference" and to reexamine how Asian American writings have been received in the discussion of U.S. multiculturalism and what needs to be further acknowledged in order to fully appreciate the open perspective of multiculturalism. Recent attention to Asian American writings suggests the usefulness of questioning how the literature written by Asian Americans has been received by mainstream literary markets and to what extent its newfound status among the multicultural literature represents the reality of, and voice for, minorities and immigrants in the United States. If literature written by Asian immigrants (or their descendents) is treated as a mere "their" literature that "our" Americans might need to appreciate in the context of multicultural diversity, the inclusion of much Asian American literature in the American literary canon would be a mere pretense and, in effect, a disguised expression of dominant Americanism. Such a literature so produced and consumed might also lead us to rethink what multicultural society needs to undertake.

The division of this book into two parts is intended to emphasize the two contrasting stances that Asian American writers have taken. If politically acquiescent multicultural representations, whether in literature or in other media, have occupied a "popular" and dominant place in the cultural apprehension of multiculturalism, politically conscious multiculturalism has by contrast been relatively marginalized in the reception of multicultural literature. Stated plainly, the dominant culture has celebrated model immigrants' success stories. By contrast, the voices of dissidence and distance from the dominant American culture and politics have received little attention from readers and literary markets. While Part I focuses on how the politically disengaging voice has become a dominant representation of Asian American literature and examines the ideology of a "model minority," Part II concerns the counterpart to the politically acquiescent Asian American multiculturalism and proposes an oppositional and alternative reading of multicultural Asian American literature involving a critical awareness of being a "minority" in the United States.

Chapter One seeks to demystify the ideology of Asian Americans as a "model minority" and examines politically acquiescent attitudes pervasive in Asian Americans. I attempt to show how the Immigration Act of 1965 has fostered the "success" myth of Asian immigrants; how Asian immigrants have been discriminated against for their race or ethnicity in terms of wage and equal opportunities, which is a renewed yet continued exploitation of racial/ethnic minorities; and how the earlier middlemen status of Asian immigrants, who are seen as "docile" and "useful" in the U.S. economy, is still continued in the form of "modern-day high-tech coolies."

Chapter Two analyzes some Asian American multicultural texts that have been widely circulated and registered by readers as "popular" Asian American writings. I will focus on three of the most commercially successful—Jade Snow Wong's *Fifth Chinese Daughter* (1950), Maxine Hong Kingston's *The Woman Warrior* (1976), and Amy Tan's *Joy Luck*

Club (1989). Although much research on these popular writings has been done, it seems necessary to consider what elements in their writings have appealed to readers and how the literary works became popular in the context of U.S. multiculturalism. I will also examine whether these writers have voluntarily conformed to the taste of non-Asian readers by means of commodifying "Oriental" cultures, or whether some aesthetic elements in these writings have been used for marketability and thus ironically have helped to commodify and essentialize cultural differences. If these writings are widely received for their "exotic" cultural elements regardless of the writers' intention, then the concept of U.S. multiculturalism suggested in Asian American writings needs to be reexamined, because the "cultural diversity" that U.S. multiculturalism celebrates has eventually contributed to reinforcing the image of Asian Americans as "Orientals," or essentially different.

Part Two gives greater attention to political and economic contexts of the immigration of Asian immigrants and their position in U.S. society. Introduction of nonwhites to the United States, construction of racist ideologies, and exclusionary immigration policies—all are closely connected to the process of U.S. development of capitalism. In a similar manner, the lives of immigrants and racial minorities in the United States have been constantly and continuously changed, oscillating with the changes of U.S. political economy and legal policies. The use of Chinese workers as cheap labor as well as a "union-dissolving force," the exploitation of the colonized as a "reserve army" of U.S. labor markets, and the ongoing global restructuring of U.S. capitalism within and outside the nation also reflect how racial and ethnic minorities have been purposely used and exploited in the struggle between capital and labor occurring in the developmental process of capitalism. Either as free laborers or as colonized bodies, Asian immigrants have been used as middlemen in domestic and international contexts of global capitalism. Contexualizing the issues of structural contradiction and political and ideological crises in the capitalist system, Part II introduces the dissident voice against U.S.-centered capitalist expansionism and the socioeconomic and political mechanisms that have scapegoated immigrants in the United States.

Chapter Three seeks to move beyond the ethnicity-oriented approach to Asian American literature in order to pay more attention to the socioeconomic mechanism that has systematically discriminated minority immigrants along race/ethnicity lines. The migration of racial/ethnic minorities, the utilization of their labor at cheap wage, and the tension between racial/ethnic immigrants and domestic workers are all part of a historical process occurring in conflicts between capital and labor in the capitalist system. Filipinos' migration in the 1930s provides an example of how the colonized

have become an internal colonial labor force and how they have been utilized as a reserve army for U.S. labor markets, which is similar to what
Puerto Ricans are currently experiencing. Carlos Bulosan's *America Is In
The Heart* (1946) portrays how racially and nationally oppressed immigrants have been exploited as cheap labor in U.S. labor markets.

Although the Immigration Act of 1965 has abolished legal discrimination against Asian immigrants, inequality and unequal power relations
along race/ethnicity lines in U.S. labor markets have continued throughout history. In fact, labor exploitation and racial/ethnic stratification and
conflicts among ethnic communities have increased, and recent changes
of ethnic compositions within communities reveal an example of how the
ongoing restructuring of U.S. capitalism has racially and ethnically stratified immigrants and exploited their labor. Fae Myenne Ng's *Bone* (1993)
is a narrative of the stratified racial/ethnic composition and the continuing
economic utilization of labor along racial/ethnic minorities, which eventually demystifies the "success" myth of Asian immigrants/Asian Americans.
Both Bulosan and Ng focus on how Asian immigrants have been politically, economically, and ideologically used in domestic labor markets, and
they interrogate the manner in which social and economic mechanisms and
restrictive legal policies have been practiced against Asian immigrants in
the United States.

Chapter Four inquires into whether there is any "essential" component of Asian American literature, or whether Asian American writers
"should" reflect ethnicity-specific issues through their writings. This chapter
challenges the "ethnicity-oriented" approach to Asian American literature.
Karen Tei Yamashita's *Tropic of Orange* (1997) represents a questioning
of the essentialized discourse of Asian American literary representations as
well as white-dominant views of Asian American literature as "essentially
different" or "exotic," as found in most commercially successful Asian
American writings. *Tropic of Orange* is in a way Yamashita's revising of
U.S. multicultural/racial society from the marginalized perspective. In analyzing Yamashita's critical Asian American multicultural text, this chapter
seeks to emphasize the structural contradiction in the U.S. capitalist system
and U.S. ambivalent treatment of racial/ethnic minorities, and it argues for
moving beyond the superficial understanding of racial/ethnic differences or
cultural diversity.

Chapter Five attempts to dismantle hierarchical paradigms of us/them
and Self/other projected towards Asian American literature, analyzing Ruth
Ozeki's *My Year of Meats* (1998) in order to show an example of critical Asian American multicultural writing resistant to the white middle-class
dominant perspective. Ozeki's *My Year of Meats* presents an alternative

vision of "American" identity and portrays an image of multicultural/racial American reality from the underrepresented racial/ethnic minority's perspective. In the same manner that minority immigrants have been economically exploited and ideologically utilized in U.S. labor markets, Ozeki portrays how biracial identity has been utilized for mediating cultural and economic commodities in international and transnational capitalist contexts. Ozeki's subversive strategy of turning the white middle-class dominant gaze onto racial/ethnic minorities is indeed her resistance to the contradictory U.S. rhetoric and the structural inequality practiced against racial/ethnic minorities in the United States.

My central contention in this book is that more productive means of analysis must be brought to the understanding of Asian American writings by means of raising consciousness about the politicizing effects of U.S. multiculturalism. Although U.S. multiculturalism has revealed its own limitations, the appreciation of multicultural literary works also becomes possible by means of revising the limits and stretching the definition of U.S. multiculturalism. Ultimately one must recognize that there is a need for more critical Asian American multicultural texts in order to fully appreciate the "democratic" meaning of diversity as well as to foreground the specific contexts of economic disruption, social marginalization, and labor exploitation that Asian immigrants have experienced in the development of U.S. capitalism.

Part One
Politically Acquiescent Asian American Multiculturalism

Many Asian American writings have been published in the form of autobiography, biography, or *Bildungsroman,* and generational gaps and cultural differences expressed by the descendents of the immigrant generation have to some degree furnished the typifying subject of "ethnic" literature. Racial/ethnic minorities' personal struggles to find their identity in the United States, alongside their perceived "success" stories, were regarded moreover as "model minority" discourse. Although many Asians born in the United States have been socially integrated and culturally assimilated to U.S. culture and are legally American citizens, most literary works presented by Asian American writers have been understood within hierarchical binaries of us/them, Self/Other, First world/Third world, and familiar/exotic. The hierarchical perspective in effect differentiates "Americans" internally into colored races.

The way ethnic differences are spectacularized as "exotic" reflects the unequal power relations existing in society. White ethnicity has not been labeled an "exotic" culture in the United States, and in the same paradigm the term "exotic" is ideologically and commercially manufactured in reference to racial/ethnic "minorities" from the white dominant perspective. In other words, "exotic" refers to cultural "otherness," and this perceived difference of cultural others is projected from the racially and ethnically white European dominant perspective. In effect, the perspective of Asian American literature as "exotic" representations of "culturally different others" is the product of Western-oriented hierarchical conceptions. Despite exoticism not being an inherent quality found in a certain culture or people, most Asian American writings were perceived as "exotic" cultural representations. Mainstream white middle-class dominant perspectives on ethnic

13

differences as "exotic" are an extension of hierarchical paradigms based on unequal power relations, much as the history of men's voyeurism of women implies an unequal power relation.

The white dominant perspective on Asian Americans as "culturally different others" has significantly influenced the production of Asian American literary works. Some Asian American writers' projection of a white-dominant point of view reflects an internalization of the hierarchical value system without questioning its effects. In some ways, ethnic differences rendered by Asian American writers have been instrumentalized to denote cultural otherness from the white dominant hierarchical perspective, and the difference furthermore has been exaggerated to fix Asian Americans as essentially different others. While ethnic writers of white European descent seemed to have virtually no boundaries to the subject matter of their literary representations, descendents of non-whites such as Asians have actually focused on issues surrounding their ethnicity and related subjects. It also needs to be considered whether Asian American writers have highlighted the ethnic difference for reasons of commercial appeal, or if there was an influence in terms of mainstream publisher's demand for the production of "ethnic" literature by racial/ethnic minorities.

My main interest here is the political and ideological stance that Asian American writers have shown through their writings. The contrast I have made between the politically acquiescent and the politically conscious Asian American multicultural writings is intended to focus attention on whether racial/ethnic minority writers demonstrate an awareness of unequal power relations along race/ethnicity lines, or whether they allow themselves to be projected as cultural "others," while conforming to existing unequal power relations and seeking a commercial appeal for their writings. The position of Asian American writers in this regard reveals either that they consciously react to subvert the unequal power structure embedded in hierarchical encoding of racial/ethnic identity, or they participate conversely in perpetuating the ethnic difference by commodifying it as "exotic."

Thus, it is important to discern to what extent the so-called "popular" minority writers' success has been related to the commodified perception of cultural otherness. The reason Asian Americans are depicted as "essentially" different "cultural others," if one follows Leith Mullings's definition, is that "the cognitive component of ethnicity," is being highlighted instead of the "social structural component of ethnicity."[1] Mullings's "cognitive component of ethnicity" is indeed highlighted in most "popular" Asian American literary works. The stereotypical image of Asian Americans/Asian immigrants as "exotic others" is a further extension of the cognitive component of ethnicity-oriented perspective in defining identity. This approach, according to Mullings, downplays unequal "social relations" at structural levels and masks the actual discrimination working against racial/ethnic minorities.

The "popular" Asian American multicultural writings have also shown politically disengaging attitudes, while celebrating success stories of assimilation. Most "popular" Asian American writings have not grounded the texts in specific historical and political contexts. Rather, they have avoided highlighting the contradictory rhetoric that the United States government has taken toward immigrants throughout its history. Instead, most "popular" Asian American writers have foregrounded cultural/ethnic differences at the descriptive level and in many ways the difference was spectacularized as "exotic." The ambivalence, or the double strategy in my view, that most "popular" Asian American writers have taken reflects the fact that many of them are politically conservative and conforming. They allow themselves to be projected as cultural others, yet seek for a "commercial appeal" through "exoticized" differences.

Jeffery Paul Chan, Frank Chin, Lawson Fusao Inada, and Shawn Hsu Wong point out that many Asian American works, especially by Chinese American women writers, have been "silent" about the unequal power structure in society. Chan and the others make the criticism that many Chinese American writings have reaffirmed the "same old white Christian fantasy of little Chinese victims of 'the original sin of being born to a brutish, sadomasochistic culture of cruelty and victimization' fleeing to America in search of freedom from everything Chinese and seeking white acceptance."[2] The writers and literary works they criticize are Yung Wing's *My Life in China and America* (1909); Leong Gor Yun's *Chinatown Inside Out* (1936); Pardee Lowe's *Father and Glorious Descendent* (1943); Jade Snow Wong's *Fifth Chinese Daughter* (1950); Virginia Lee's *The House that Tai Ming Built* (1963); Chuang Hua's *Crossing* (1968); Betty Lee Sung's *Mountain Gold* (1972); Maxine Hong Kingston's *The Woman Warrior* (1976), *China Men* (1980), and *Tripmaster Monkey* (1989); and Amy Tan's *The Joy Luck Club* (1989).[3] The criterion Chan and the others set up for "good" Asian American writing is how "real" was the depiction of Chinese history and culture in their stories.[4] I do not entirely agree with Chan and the others' method of treating Chinese American women writers' literary works as totally conforming ideologically, nor with their argument for "real" (fact-based) Chinese culture depicted in Chinese American literature. To my thinking their argument itself is leading toward establishing an essentializing discourse of Asian American writing.

Despite my disagreement with Chan and the others' criterion, some of the points they have made regarding the politically conservative and disengaging voice embedded in many Chinese (or Asian) American writings are worth noting. They suggest that the silent conformism present in most "popular" Asian American writings ironically reveals the impressive extent to which white racism has maintained its dominance.[5] A criticism offered by Chan and the others is that many Asian (Chinese) American women writers have conformed to the stereotype that white dominant society has set up for them and "live" and "talk" within the "bounds of the stereotype" without questioning.[6] What they point out is that the image of Asian Americans as a "model minority" is another "racist tactic" by which the United States induces the assimilation, acculturation, or silence of Asian Americans. This image implies the potential extent to which Asian Americans have "paid a price" for their survival through being silent, and how their silence has been ideologically disguised with the label "model minority." Criticizing Asian American literature's tendency to reproduce the stereotype created by the white dominant "American" society, Chan and the others argue that most "popular" Asian American literary works have conformed to the predominantly white readership's expectation of, and the publisher's demands for, "ethnic" literature.

The stereotypical image of Asian Americans as a "model minority," created by white dominant society, is in a sense very similar to the function of the term "exotic" within hierarchical paradigms. Just as the "exotic" is an ideologically and commercially coined tag referring to cultural minorities within white dominant, unequal power relations, the label of Asian Americans as a "model minority" has been ideologically and politically manufactured in order to maintain the system, while putting one racial/ethnic minority as a "model" before the others.

In many ways, the role of publishing companies has been an important element in the production, distribution, and evaluation of multicultural literary works. The publishers' main purpose is to satisfy mainstream readers' tastes as well as to fulfill their commercial interest by producing books that appeal to the general public. Publishers also have influenced people's way of looking at other cultures by channeling literary production in specific directions. Some "popular" Asian American writers who have participated in reproducing the existing stereotype of minorities delineate with a politically conservative voice the circumstances in which immigrants or racial/ethnic minorities have been situated in the United States, thus contributing to the commodifying of their ethnic culture as "exotic oriental." If the "popular" model minority discourse avoids socio-economic and political tensions that impact racial minorities, the silence—whether it was forced or not—indicates the writers' political stance. Whether the multicultural literary works of Asian Americans contribute to reinforcing the dominant cultural discourse on "minority" literature or play the role of a counter-hegemonic discourse depends on whether these writers try to work within the existing stereotypical representation or try to subvert dominant codes and demystify the ideologies.

If Asian American literature functions as a mere "ethnic" literature by reproducing a typical image engraved on Asians, those narratives eventually function as an "exotic commodity" and their cultural, racial, or ethnic differences become "essentialized." If Asian American writers participate in essentializing ethnic differences as "exotic," then a question arises: For whose sake is multiculturalism promoted and celebrated? If minority writers cannot speak for themselves, it ironically induces us to reassess the current level of U.S. multiculturalism, which is pervasive yet does not speak for racial/ethnic minorities. As a way of questioning hierarchical perspectives in reading Asian American literature in the light of U.S. multiculturalism, as well as of examining the ideologically ambivalent position in which Asian American immigrants have been situated in U.S. labor markets, the next chapter discusses the socioeconomic and political background of the creation of the "model minority" ideology and seeks to demystify the "success" myth of Asian Americans, who are circumscribed in their position as economic middlemen in U.S. society while being politically disempowered.

Chapter One
Cultural Economies of Model Minority Creation

This chapter focuses on how the United States has used Asian immigrants as a source of cheap labor as well as a force to bring stability in the face of political, economic, and ideological crisis occurring in capitalism's development. I am primarily taking Chinese immigrants as an example, although other groups of Asian immigrants have confronted similar problems. As the first Asian immigrant laborers to the United States, the Chinese have faced economic exploitation as well as social and legal exclusion from society, and the historical story of Chinese immigrants elucidates a central part of the problem that I am seeking to address in this book.

Although it is widely acknowledged that immigrants from Asia have contributed to sustaining U.S. society, there was little attention paid to why the U.S. government or U.S.-based corporations recruited people from different cultural and racial backgrounds, or from the U.S. colonies, or to how immigrants have been used as cheap laborers as well as a convenient target to be blamed for economic depression and unemployment. Throughout history, the United States has used the cheap labor force of immigrants from various countries while changing the labor sources to accord with U.S. foreign policies or economic circumstances. The forced introduction of Africans as slaves, the migration of European immigrants, the recruitment of Chinese and Mexicans to replace African Americans as well as European immigrants, reveal the conflicting but consistent pursuit of capitalist employers' never-ending effort to get more profits by means of cheaper labor resources.

From the capitalist perspective, immigrant workers were cheaper labor sources, but they were also used as a means of dissolving the unified labor force. One way of dissolving labor resources has been to use different immigrant workers and circulate racist ideology. In *U.S. Immigration Law and the Control of Labor: 1820–1924*, Kitty Calavita interprets the migration of labor as a part of capitalist structure and emphasizes how capitalists have used persons of color or immigrants as a force for breaking down organized labor unions. Many Asian immigrants had no conception of what a strike was and they were at first unaware of their place in it. Soon immigrants realized that employers were using them to break down labor unions by giving them lower wages than other domestic white workers and thus threaten labor organization. From the capitalists' perspective, unionization of labor is the biggest threat to survival, and the hiring of flexible cheap immigrant labor is a way of avoiding conflict between labor workers and employers. The reason that the U.S. economy has heavily depended on immigrant laborers is found in the economical and ideological advancement of capitalist interests. Because their status is unstable, immigrants are especially vulnerable to the consequences of being fired by employers whenever workers unionize or demand their rights. As Calavita has remarked,

> Immigration . . . can be seen not just as an economically and ideologically useful tool to capital, but an ideal temporary solution to dilemmas derived from the most fundamental contradiction in capitalism, the class contradiction, for immigration allows increased levels of exploitation both by providing access to a virtually unlimited supply of labor and by introducing a potentially divisive element into the working class.[1]

Hence, Calavita points out that the reason for introducing immigrant labor was to "maximize the profit" as well as to "stabilize the system."[2] In other words, Asian immigrant workers have been exploited by employers and rejected by white American workers and their society.

Looking back at the history of immigration, there were more European immigrant workers than Asian immigrants in the beginning, and government officials encouraged immigration. Immigrants were to supply the cheap labor necessary for the advancement of industry in the United States. In 1921, this policy of encouraging immigration was reversed when European immigrant workers quickly unionized to protect their rights. The militant unionization movement became a national issue and led capitalists to pursue other sources of labor.

Chinese were actively recruited to replace the European immigrants when they became unionized to protect their rights.[3] Chinese were the first Asian immigrants recruited by the labor agencies. They were actively recruited to fill needs in railroad construction, mining, and domestic service, and their labor could be purchased at much lower wages than other white workers' labor. As an alternative labor power to substitute for European immigrant laborers, Chinese were used by capitalists as a union-disintegrating force.

> In 1870 the Crispins at Sampson's shoe factory struck. They demanded higher wages, end of the ten-hour day, access to the company's books in order to fix wages in accordance with profits, and the discharge of workers delinquent in their dues to the Crispin organization. Sampson fired the striking workers. Unsuccessful in his effort to hire scabs from a nearby town, he decided to declare total war against the Crispins and drive a "wedge" into the conflict. The "wedge" was a contingent of Chinese workers from San Francisco. A year before the Crispin strike against Sampson's factory, the official organ of shoe manufacturers, *Hide and Leather Interest,* had condemned the Crispins and urged employers to import Chinese workers as strikebreakers. Meanwhile, Sampson had read a newspaper article on the effective use of Chinese labor in a San Francisco shoe factory, and sent his superintendent there to sign a contract with a Chinese contract-labor company.[4]

It is known that by using Chinese labor the owner saved the factory $40,000 in the first year and helped break the union. This incident received widespread attention in the Northeast, contributing to labor's antagonism towards Chinese immigrants while helping to make Chinese exclusion a national rather than regional issue.[5] White employers often favorably compared the Chinese to striking European immigrant workers, but European immigrant workers perceived the Chinese as a "subservient" and "compliant" labor force and did not think that Chinese workers could have a working-class consciousness and establish solidarity with domestic white workers and European immigrant workers. Rather, they viewed the Chinese as a threatening force.[6] Chinese workers were depicted by employers as "docile" employees compared to striking domestic whites and European immigrant workers. The effect of this "docile" image of the Chinese was to dissociate them from other domestic proletariat and European immigrant workers.

CHINESE LABORERS AS "COOLIES"

Historically, Chinese laborers were recruited after slavery was abolished and came to the United States as free laborers. However, they were often called "coolies," which denotes "unfree laborers who had been kidnapped or pressed to service by coercion and shipped to foreign countries."[7] Although they were free to sell their labor, the Chinese were separated by boundaries of race and ethnicity and they were differently stratified from the domestic white proletariat laborers. The term indeed has been racially constructed to define the Chinese as cheap labor in the U.S. labor market. Robert Lee has explained,

> The Chinese who immigrated to the United States as laborers arrived, in fact, as free labor in both the legal and the economic sense. However, once here, Chinese workers became intensely proletarianized and racially excluded "coolies." The designation of hiring labor as "coolie labor," like its analog "nigger work," racialized the meaning of common labor.[8]

As Lee points out, the term "coolies" denotes the doubly exploited Chinese laborers, who were ideologically and economically utilized in the U.S. labor market and racially excluded from the society. Just as African slaves were replaced by Chinese laborers after slavery was legally abolished, the status of the Chinese was in line with a transformation from "chattel slaves" into "wage slaves" in the U.S. labor market.[9]

Furthermore, legal restriction on the Chinese put them into a vulnerable position like "indentured laborers." Chinese were not allowed to apply for U.S. citizenship due to the restrictive U.S. immigration policies enacted against non-whites since 1870, and their limited legal status as sojourners made them hard to unionize as a group because they could be fired or deported at any time when employers found out about their labor unionization. Legal exclusions and racism against Chinese workers have eventually prevented them from establishing solidarity with other domestic white workers and European immigrants. Despite Chinese laborers being racially and ethnically differentiated in the U.S. labor market, the status of the Chinese as cheap labor has been regarded as threatening to other domestic working classes. Lee in this sense calls the first wave Chinese workers, who replaced the striking European and domestic laborers, a "nineteenth-century model minority"—a "middlemen" position that was ironically assigned by white domestic employers.[10]

Although images of the Chinese as "subservient," "compliant," or as a "union-breaking" middlemen minority were widespread, the idea of calling for fair working conditions—"free men, not coolies"—was actually raised among Chinese laborers, and 8000 Chinese railroad builders went on strike on June 25, 1867. Chinese workers demanded equal labor and wage conditions with white workers and asked for the increase of their wage from $40 to $45 a month. The strike lasted for a week, but was forced to stop due to shortage of food and water, which was cut by Crocker, the director of the railroad.[11] This historical event is also well described in Kingston's *China Men.*

> The China Men, then, decided go on strike and demand forty-five dollars a month and the eight-hour shift. They risked going to jail and the Central Pacific keeping the pay it was banking for them. Ah Goong memorized the English, "Forty-five dollars a month—eight-hour shift." He practiced the strike slogan: "Eight hours a day good for white man, all the same good for China Man."[12]

Despite the Chinese fight for fair treatment and equal wages while unionizing their labor force, the strike failed and Chinese workers did not receive treatment equal to other white domestic workers and European immigrant workers. Although there was more labor movement organized by Chinese in the 1870s, the Chinese labor unionization movement is not well known to the American public.[13]

During the recession in the later 1870s, whites competed with Chinese for jobs, and Chinese became the targets of violence and were driven out of small towns and villages and sought refuge in large cities.[14] This racial prejudice, exacerbated by fear of competition from aliens, prompted calls for restrictive federal immigration laws. Anti-coolie clubs sprang up, and sporadic boycotts of Chinese-made goods followed.[15] Chinese exclusion was first enacted in 1882, and a small number of Japanese began arriving in the 1880s. The commencement of Japanese immigration corresponds to the period of Chinese exclusion in that Japanese came in substantial numbers in the 1890s, a period of Chinese decline. At the height of the Chinese exclusion movement, agricultural labor demand in Hawaii and California led to increased efforts to attract Japanese workers. Like the Chinese, Japanese laborers were warmly welcomed by employers. But by the turn of the century, unfavorable sentiment toward the Japanese grew, as their laborers began to migrate to the mainland of the United States.[16] The restrictive immigration policy against the Japanese was enacted through the Gentlemen's Agreement in 1904, and it eventually stopped the flow of Japanese immigrants to the United States. Many Asian immigrants came to face hostile reactions of multiple kinds from the surrounding population, including riots, anti-Asian legislation, and, ultimately, exclusion laws or efforts to prohibit further immigration. Various restrictive immigration laws against Asians and racist rhetoric such as "servile coolie" or "unassimilable inferior race" have reinforced the maintenance of the status of minority immigrants as the "forever alien" in the United States.

Whereas capital has maximized its profits by using racially and culturally different immigrants as cheap labor, restrictive immigration laws have bound the status of immigrant laborers and eventually have helped employers to exploit the unstable and "disposable" immigrants. In other words, immigration policies have created and implemented a legal solution to domestic economic and labor problems.[17] The recent changes in U.S. immigration policies (especially the reformed Immigration Act of 1965) reveal another example of how the United States has managed the political, economic, or ideological crisis by using the different groups of immigrants, by hierarchizing them, and by letting them build racial tension against each other in the postwar era.

If Asian immigrants before the Immigration Act of 1965 were mostly unskilled laborers and legally categorized as "unassimilable" aliens, the Immigration Act of 1965, which formally abolished the prohibition against Asians, announced a new pattern of immigration allowing an annual quota of 20,000 from each Asian country. The passage of the Immigration Act of 1965 occurred in an international context, because the relations between the United States and Asia after the Cold War have undergone a tremendous change in a form of transnational economic trade.

Since the immigration quotas after the 1965 immigration policy were given mostly to skilled laborers (professionals) or people who have capital to invest in the United States, the domestic "racialization" of Asian immigrants has been differently stratified compared to other immigrant groups. Although after 1975 large numbers of people, especially from countries such as Vietnam, Laos, and Cambodia, came to the United States as political refugees with no economic means, recent comers from Asian countries, especially from the Philippines, Taiwan, India, China, Japan, and Korea, were mostly middle-class professionals, students, or investors, and they formed a different class, thus creating internal layers among Asian Americans. In spite of the large numbers of Asian immigrants who are still struggling with poverty, the problem of the poverty of these immigrants has been underrepresented. Only the overall image of Asian immigrants as a "successful" minority is widespread in American society while causing some tension with other racial minorities. Previous racial tensions occurred between whites and blacks or majority and minority, following the media's stereotyping of Asians as a middle class, but racial tension within the United States has slowly changed toward conflict between Asian Americans and Chicano/Latino Americans, or between Asian Americans and African Americans or even within interethnic groups.

Although Asian immigrants were "yellow proletariat"[18] in the nineteenth century and are now called a "middle-class model minority," the middlemen status of Asian immigrants as a force for breaking labor union-ism or as a "model" for other minorities has been continuously used to serve the needs of U.S. capitalism and political as well as ideological pur-poses. The ambivalent position of Asian immigrants transitioned from "coolies" to "modern-day high-tech coolies"[19] has not been much changed in terms of how they have served U.S. capitalist development and ideologi-cal stabilization while supplying their cheap labor.

"MODERN DAY HIGH-TECH COOLIES" AS A "MODEL MINORITY"

The middlemen position that the Chinese were straddling in the 1870s as a "union-dissolving force" is reverberating again for twentieth-century Asian Americans. White "American" society has labeled Asian Americans as a "model" compared to African Americans and Chicanos/Latino Americans and touted Asians' economic "success" and achievement without any help from government, while contrasting African Americans and Chicanos/ Latino Americans as "aid-depending" racial minorities. Although the his-torical context of the first wave Chinese immigrants is not exactly the same as the modern day Asian immigrants, the ambivalent position of Asian immigrants in U.S. society as middlemen—either as favorable employees compared to other domestic labor strikers and European immigrants, or as a "self-serving" minority compared to African Americans and Chicanos/ Latino Americans—has not changed much.

The portrayal of Asian Americans as a "successful" minority seems to have begun in the mid-1960s with depictions in the press of Japanese Americans who had gone through the harsh racist reality of internment years, yet survived through their hard work. The media also used the term "model minority" in order to refer to the "success" that Chinese Americans had achieved without relying on government welfare. As one news report phrased the situation in 1966:

> At a time when Americans are awash in worry over the plight of racial minorities—One such minority, the nation's 300,000 Chinese-Ameri-cans, is winning wealth and respect by dint of its own hard work. In any Chinatown from San Francisco to New York, you discover young-sters at grips with their studies. Crime and delinquency are found to be rather minor in scope. Still being taught in Chinatown is the old idea that people should depend on their own efforts—not a welfare check— in order to reach America's "promised land." . . . At a time when it is being proposed that hundreds of billions be spent to uplift Negroes and

other minorities, the nation's 300,000 Chinese-Americans are moving
ahead on their own—with no help from anyone else.[20]

The above account implies that Chinese Americans achieved great success
by overcoming discrimination with diligence and high aspirations for education. In other words, the comments attribute the "success" of Chinese
Americans to their work ethic and behavior. By focusing on individuals'
efforts to succeed, the image of Asians as a "model minority" has helped
American society justify its structural inequality and reaffirm the underlying structure by shifting the minority problem to individuals and communities rather than allowing for an examination of the unequal power
structure of the society. The label "model minority" pinned on Chinese and
Japanese Americans has extended to Asian Americans in general.[21] However, the notion of an Asian American "model minority" has been conten-
tious ever since its inception.

"Success" stories of Asian immigrants, which praise their behavior modes, seem to target other nonwhite minorities. The image of Asian
immigrants who have "succeeded" without getting any government help
has been used to criticize other racial minorities, because at that time it
was being proposed that hundreds of billions be spent to "uplift" other
minorities. The media depiction of Asian immigrants as a "model minority" has concealed the racist reality and unequal power structure that have
prevented minorities from improving themselves and also helped the U.S.
to justify its myth as a "land of promise," which implies that everybody
can make their wish come true depending on individuals' efforts, regardless
of their race, gender, and class backgrounds. Also, the widespread image
of Asian Americans as a "model minority" has led them to be dissociated
from other racial minorities, who were still struggling with poverty, racial
discrimination, and social oppression and it has eventually put Asian Americans in a straitened position between whites and blacks, or blacks and Chi-
canos/Latino Americans.

However, while emphasizing cultural and ethnic values as factors
in the economic "success" of Asian Americans, the media stereotype of
Asian Americans as a "model minority" did not explain the structural
changes that have altered the racial context significantly since the Immigration Act of 1965. The demographic change of Asian Americans actually occurred with the Immigration Act of 1965, and the migration of
Asians has dramatically increased since then. Morrison Wong in his
article, "Post-1965 Asian Immigrants," says that in the pre-1965 period,
Asian immigration accounted for only about 8 percent of the total immigrant population, about 22,000 immigrants per year. From 1965 to 1981,

Asian immigration increased almost tenfold; there was a substantial increase from each Asian country except Japan. In the most recent period, about 235,000 Asian immigrants, about 43 percent of the total immigrant population, entered the United States each year.[22] Although it was the time in which the second and third generation of Chinese and Japanese immigrants emerged as a middle class, the preference-based Immigration Act of 1965 has changed the composition of Asians, because the new immigrants were mostly relatives of U.S. citizens, investors, professionals or students especially in the area of science and technology. In addition, recent Asian immigrants (with the exception of refugees from Vietnam, Laos and Cambodia) have actually brought capital, skills or economic means with them.

The change of immigration policies and the lifting of regulations on Asian immigrants have not proceeded from the benevolence of U.S. policies. Rather, the changes in U.S. immigration policies are the consequence of the U.S. involvement in Asian wars and development of the capitalism of Asian countries such as the Philippines, Vietnam, China, Taiwan, Japan, and Korea, as well as the emergence of transnational capitalism. As John Liu and Lucie Cheng have noted, the United States, "to safeguard its interests and to prevent the Soviet Union from gaining the upper hand, . . . began laying the foundations for the economic relations that would channel the flow of capital, technology, and people between Asia and itself."[23] According to their analysis, the United States accomplished its ends "by underwriting the reconstruction of selected parts of war-torn Asia."[24] In other words, the underlying reason that the United States eased the restriction on Asians in 1965 was to pave a way for binding U.S. political and economic relations with Asian countries. Also, the capitalist development of Asian countries under U.S. influence after World War II and the export-oriented economies of these countries have fostered the infusion of foreign capital and technology, and skilled laborers have been pushed to migrate to the United States as a result of the widespread ideology of the United States as a "land of opportunity" as well as the influence of U.S. educational systems on Asian countries.[25] Liu and Cheng point out:

> Pervasive U.S. involvement in the post World War II restructuring of the Asian Pacific regional political economy established the conditions for both professional/skilled and semiskilled/unskilled worker immigration. The rise of capitalist ideology and the articulation of U.S. and Asian educational systems provided the basic motivation and opportunities for emigration. Highly publicized success stories of Asian immigrants helped sustain the motivation of other potential emigrants.[26]

Although some Asian professionals were U.S.-born, the majority (76.8 percent) immigrated from abroad, primarily from the Philippines, India, mainland China, Taiwan, Japan, and Korea.[27] Despite skilled or professional Asian immigrants being touted as a "model minority," they have actually faced racial discrimination in terms of wages and career opportunities.

> The land of opportunity is far more limited than they had expected, and, contrary to what they have been taught, meritocracy is not color blind. Many seek to compensate for their race by outperforming their peers. Working longer hours and carrying out jobs beyond the call of duty, they ironically provide support for the "model minority" stereotype and harden the glass ceiling.[28]

What they have realized is that they are perceived as "modern-day high-tech coolies."[29] Just as the first wave of Chinese workers was favorably received by white employers as a "model" to labor-striking white domestic workers and European immigrant workers—even while they were being treated as "coolies" with lower wage than other domestic workers—ambivalent treatment of Asian immigrants has been repeated in the twentieth century.

Just as the pattern of acceptance and rejection of racial minorities has been repeated in U.S. history, so has the image of Asian immigrants transitioned from "coolies" to "high-tech coolies" or from "yellow perils" to a "model minority" and later to a threatening group from the perspective of African-Americans, Chicanos, white Americans, and interestingly, domestic college students. However, the change in labels and economic status over time has not actually brought a big difference to the situation of Asian immigrants—the "middlemen" minority in U.S. society. Nor has the economically "successful" image of Asian immigrants overridden the racial barriers that Asian Americans have experienced in U.S. society. Anti-Asian sentiment still grew even while Asian immigrants were touted as a "model minority," and backlash against Asian immigrants has occurred in more subtle ways. Anti-Asian sentiment became visible in the 1980s when Asian students enrolled in the University of California were revealed to be an over-represented group. Ronald Takaki speaks to the problem of inter-racial tensions in California in his book *Strangers From A Different Shore*. Takaki tells this story:

> In December 1986, University of California President David Gardner addressed the controversy in an interview with the San Diego Union. He pointed out that Asian-American students were over-represented in the University: Asians made up only 6 percent of the State's population, but

they comprised more than 20 percent of UC's undergraduate enrollment. Gardner explained that efforts to redress earlier ethnic imbalances for blacks and Hispanics were being jeopardized by the new Asian Americans presence. This change in the ethnic composition of the students was "causing unrest among some groups, including whites who [were] experiencing a decline in representation."[30]

Gardner, through his address, pitted Asian Americans against other racial minorities and whites, and his remarks initiated a link between issues of Asian American admissions and affirmative action, which later exploded into a political issue in California. Indeed, Asian immigrants as "middlemen" in the U.S. society work as a "buffer between whites and blacks, who are separated by not only racial difference but a related class antagonism as well."[31] The pattern of inclusion and exclusion, which has repeated itself throughout U.S. history, has been directed again against the "model" Asian Americans in more subtle and indirect ways in the postwar era.

In addition, the Immigration Act of 1965 has actually helped to form a racial and class stratification within minority communities, and the reform policy has brought a structural change. Besides the migration of professionals, skilled laborers and students, recent Asian immigrants have mostly become small-business owners of groceries or ethnic restaurants, having brought capital to invest under the visa category of investors. This was an alternative way for them to resettle in the United States. Although most of those who came to the U.S. were in the middle class and had no previous experience of running grocery stores or restaurants in their country of origin, the reasons behind their voluntary immigration in some ways reflect U.S. political, economic, and ideological influence as well as an unstable economic structure of the home country, which has been visibly or invisibly under U.S. domination, especially since World War II.

Ironically, however, the immigrants who became small business owners in the United States have assimilated the profit-oriented values of capitalism. Many Asian business owners have been hiring cheap laborers, and they have recently started hiring other immigrant workers, mostly from Latin America, at a cheap wage. Thus, labor exploitation and conflicts among racial minorities within ethnic communities have frequently occurred.[32] Recent interracial conflicts between Korean immigrants and African Americans, such as the 1992 Los Angeles "riot," or between Asian business owners and Latino workers, reveal a changing class and racial stratification among racial minorities. The pitting of racial minorities against each other, the spreading of negative stereotypes of them, or the growing interethnic as well as interracial tensions—all tell how successfully U.S. immigration laws have acted to stabilize the U.S. political, economic, and ideological system by stratifying immigrants. In this respect, the image of Asians as a "model minority" is doubly constructed in that it was first coined by the white American society to counter other minorities, and later the Immigration Act of 1965 legally structured the constitution of immigrants and their occupations in the United States while stratifying them in reference to other racial minorities.

The Immigration Act of 1965 has indeed changed racial/ethnic composition in the United States and has filtered in upper middle-class immigrants through a preference-based immigration policy. Many Asian immigrants who took advantage of the reformed policy as a chance to migrate to the United States have shown a politically disengaging, yet economically active attitude. Although Asian Americans are ideologically and economically circumscribed in terms of their economic middlemen position in the United States, many Asian Americans who have settled down as middle-class have shown a tendency to be politically silent or even disengaging about unequal power relations along race/ethnicity lines. Whether their silence is forced or not is another question. In some ways, their silence or "subservience," as Chan and the others have mentioned, could be their "price" for having escaped their politically and economically unstable countries of origin, which are under U.S. influence, and for having "successfully" resettled in the United States. On the other hand, many Asian Americans who used to be in the upper middle-class in their countries of origin already had politically conservative perspectives. Thus they interpret the ideology of a "model minority" without questions and regard it as an "honorable" label.

In fact, many Asian American writers have shown politically acquiescent attitudes through their writings while foregrounding their ethnic differences, and ironically most of them were "popularly" acknowledged as if they represent a "model" ethnic literature. In the next chapter, I analyze three "popular" Asian American writings and examine whether their popularity was made possible by following the politically conservative ideology, which in a way justifies the myth of a "model minority"; also, whether the writers' emphasis on their unique cultural experiences as racial/ethnic minorities has paradoxically helped to exaggerate the difference fixing them as "essential others"; and finally, whether their narratives of cultural differences have been commodified and exchanged as "exotic commodities."

Chapter Two
Measuring Silences in Popular Asian American Literature

> [T]he exotic is not, as is often supposed, an inherent *quality* to be found 'in' certain people, distinctive objects, or specific places; exoticism describes, rather, a particular mode of aesthetic *perception*—one which renders people, objects and places strange even as it domesticates them, and which effectively manufactures otherness even as it claims to surrender to its immanent mystery.
>
> —Gramham Huggan,
> *The Postcolonial Exotic:*
> *Marketing the Margins*

Cultural pluralism has been celebrated under the slogan of U.S. multiculturalism and its promotion of diversity. However, unequal power relations between majority whites and racial minorities have been ongoing, and in the case of minority writers entering the mainstream literary market has not been easy. These writers have had to negotiate with or serve the mainstream publishers' demands, or skillfully filter literary and political censorship through artistic devices. Graham Huggan discusses the dilemma that racial/cultural minority writers are experiencing. He explains that minority writers

> are often caught between the desire to achieve recognition with a wider audience and their awareness of the constraints this might place on their writing and the ways in which it is received. The danger exists, for example, of the edges of a certain, unmistakably politicized kind of writings becoming blunted by a coterie of publishers and other marketing agents anxious to exploit it for its 'exotic' appeal.[1]

Publishers or market-oriented culture industries have already shown a tendency to exploit cultural differences by attaching a tag, "the exotic."[2]

The dilemma that minority writers face is how to react to the publisher's demand for ethnic writings.

In a similar vein, Neil Bissoondath in *Selling Illusions* delineates the current tendency of multiculturalism to commodify "ethnic" differences and shows how this commodification eventually contributes to essentializing difference as a form of "exoticism." In Bissoondath's words,

> Multiculturalism, on the face of it, insists on diversity—and yet a case can be made that it is a diversity that depends on a vigorous conformity. Trading in the exotic, it views the individual not as a member of society at large but as a unit of a smaller group ethnically, racially, or culturally defined—a group comforted by the knowledge that it has access to familiar goods, music, etc. But this is multiculturalism at its most simplistic, and in some ways most insidious, level. It is the trade-off of the marketplace, an assurance of creature comforts in exchange for playing the ethnic game.[3]

What Huggan and Bissoondath address in common is the effect that multiculturalism has of commodifying and essentializing cultural differences while foregrounding the aestheticising discourse of exoticism, which carries the implication of a "hierarchical encoding of cultural difference."[4] If Huggan and Bissoondath are correct, and if this is typical of the way that multicultural writings are received in mainstream literary markets, then it may also urge us to examine whether U.S. multiculturalism's celebration of cultural diversity and difference is another form of international marketing to advertise the myth of America in the context of twentieth-century late capitalism. Reevaluating the socio-economic and ideological contexts that U.S. multiculturalism generates will enable us to gauge the degree of openness of American society towards racial and cultural minorities.

Literary works by Asian immigrants began entering the mainstream literary markets after World War II, and some of these works have achieved popular recognition from readers and reviewers. In the context of late capitalism, cultural differences depicted by racial and cultural minorities become highlighted to the point that the differences are actually marketed as cultural "otherness" and sold as "exotic cultural commodities."[5] Essentializing labels applied to Asian immigrants, such as "yellow peril," "unassimilable aliens," an "exotic," or a "model minority" have been continuously utilized by dominant groups and by mainstream literary markets. The problem with this ideological stereotyping of Asian immigrants is that in some cases, minority writers themselves have internalized or reproduced stereotypes through their writings. In addition, they were also encouraged by mainstream publishers to conform to the existing stereotypes, while highlighting "exotic" cultural differences as their exchange value.

It is true that unequal power relations between racial/ethnic minorities and dominant whites have infiltrated into the production of literary works. Minority writers have been dependent on mainstream publishing companies' demands for their books. Minority writers to a certain extent have to negotiate the mainstream literary markets' demands placed on minority writings. Yet the extent to which minority writers contend with or collaborate with publishing companies also indirectly indicates the writers' political stance towards "American" society. If racial/ethnic writers are obliged by publishers to highlight cultural differences to the point that the difference becomes essentialized and theatricalized as "exotic" cultural otherness, these writings in a way have paid for the "partial admission" of minority writers to the mainstream literary markets by commodifying cultural differences and ethnic values.

If Asian American literature functions as a mere minority literature by reproducing the stereotypical image that the white reading establishment has grown to expect, those narratives contribute to concealing hierarchical power structures in society, and they eventually function as "exotic cultural commodities," while selling racial and cultural ethnic differences as their marketing value. My question is whether the popularity that some Asian American writers have achieved is connected to an ideological conformism towards the mainstream literary market's demands and to politically acquiescent attitudes towards dominant power groups in society. If "popularity" simply means a massive appeal to public readers' tastes, then the representativeness of these "popular" Asian American multicultural writings needs to be reexamined. Furthermore, the assessment of how their writings became popular should be differentiated in terms of the writers' ideological stance and political awareness of Asians' marginalized status in the United States. If they garnered popularity by reinforcing dominant stereotypes of Asian Americans, those writers must have gained recognition from mainstream literary markets by commodifying their "ethnic" differences in a form of stereotypical cultural exchange. In addition, if the literature of these writers has been tolerated within the dominant power groups' encoding of minority literature as "exotic otherness," it also leads us to reevaluate the current level of U.S. multiculturalism.

FITTING INTO STEREOTYPES:
JADE SNOW WONG'S *FIFTH CHINESE DAUGHTER*

The following three literary works—Jade Snow Wong's *Fifth Chinese Daughter* (1950), Maxine Hong Kingston's *The Woman Warrior* (1976), and Amy

Tan's *The Joy Luck Club* (1989)—have been widely circulated and acknowledged by readers as "popular" Asian American writings. Wong's *Fifth Chinese Daughter* immediately rose to the bestseller list and received the Commonwealth Club's medal for Non-fiction in 1951. The book has been reprinted several times and it is estimated that about a quarter of a million had read Wong's *Fifth Chinese Daughter* by 1975.[6] In 1976 it was also made into a PBS special for the U.S. Bicentennial and was claimed as the most financially successful book ever produced by a Chinese American until Kingston's *The Woman Warrior* came out in 1976.[7] *The Woman Warrior* received the National Book Critics' Circle Award for nonfiction in 1976. The first 5000-copy edition of *The Woman Warrior* sold out overnight, and its popularity and reputation have continued. Tan's *Joy Luck Club* has also been widely acknowledged by the reading public: over four million copies were sold by 1996 and it appeared on the *New York Times* bestseller list for almost nine months. The novel has been translated into more than twenty languages and the film version of *The Joy Luck Club* helped Tan to receive popular recognition of her book.[8]

Wong's *Fifth Chinese Daughter* and Tan's *Joy Luck Club* have some commonalities in the way they entered mainstream literary markets and in terms of their political perspectives. After Japan's attack on Pearl Harbor, the Chinese, hitherto excluded as aliens in the United States, were suddenly treated as allies, and they were recognized as "fellow victims of Japan's aggression." Chinese Americans were encouraged to write "novels and personal accounts about the devastating effects of the war on China, and about the strength and resilience of the Chinese people."[9] Amy Ling also notes, "Books by American-born and Chinese-born Chinese Americans suddenly mushroomed. The former were encouraged to write by an American public eager to distinguish friend from foe; the latter were impelled by personal experiences of the horrors of war."[10] Although Chinese American writers' personal accounts of war experiences did not receive a wide recognition from readers, Wong's autobiographical *Fifth Chinese Daughter,* the publication of which was encouraged in this context, became the first book to receive widespread popular attention.

Wong has mentioned that Alice Cooper, her English teacher at Mills College, encouraged her to send her essays about San Francisco's Chinatown to magazines. Later Wong wrote an autobiographical sketch for the Californian magazine *Common Ground* in 1945, and it was eventually incorporated into *Fifth Chinese Daughter,* which was published in 1950.[11] However, it is known that Elizabeth Lawrence, the editor of the book, cut out two-thirds of the manuscript, and that Cooper was responsible for binding it together.[12] Regarding the final version of her book, Wong in an interview mentions, "Some of the things are missing that I would have wanted in. Then, you know, it's like selling to Gump's or sending to a museum. Everybody has a purpose in mind in what they're carrying out. So, you know, you kind of have to work with them."[13] Wong's response on her book reveals that she is aware of the unequal power relations between the dominant whites and racial/ethnic minorities, yet she has collaborated with the publisher or with her editor in order for her book to be accepted in mainstream literary markets. Regarding the limited opportunities that minority writers have faced, Elaine Kim notes that many early Asian American autobiographers "accepted the 'cultural bridge' role while at the same time expressing their ardent desire for acceptance in American society by any means, and under almost any conditions."[14] The question is to what extent Wong was obliged to serve the mainstream literary markets' demands for minority writings and whether the popularity Wong has gained was achieved by reproducing the existing stereotypes of Chinese Americans or by catering to the tastes of predominantly white reading groups.

When Wong's *Fifth Chinese Daughter* first came out in 1950, her book was well received by American readers.[15] However, many critics' responses were not favorable, especially where her intention and political standpoint were concerned.[16] In the late 1960s, many Asian American literary critics have criticized Wong's book for downplaying the racial discrimination that Chinese Americans have faced, while depicting Chinese Americans as a "model minority." Whereas many have criticized Wong's ideologically subservient attitude towards the mainstream literary market, Xiao-huang Yin on the other hand argues that it is important to situate Wong within the social and historical context of her time and asserts that critics and commentators should give Wong credit for her "pioneering role" in "paving the way for a new generation of Chinese American writers."[17] Considering the historical circumstances in which Chinese Americans were regarded as "unassimilable foreigners," Wong's attempt to get into the mainstream literary markets by promoting her ethnic differences is, in Yin's view, understandable. Yin has written,

> Accepting attitudes popularly ascribed to the Chinese at the time, they strove to turn their ethnic legacy into an advantage that could help them gain admission into general society. By introducing the finer qualities *inherent* in Chinese American life, they hoped to create a new image of the model minority and win greater acceptance in the mainstream world. Jade Snow Wong's *Fifth Chinese Daughter* is a representative work of such efforts.[18] (My emphasis added)

According to Yin, Wong's attempt to achieve recognition from the mainstream society by "creating a new image of model minority" reflects her keen awareness of harsh racist reality. As Wong has mentioned in the introduction to the 1989 edition, the reason she wrote *Fifth Chinese Daughter* was to create "better understanding of the Chinese culture on the part of Americans," and it is clear that Wong wrote the book for the mainstream white readership and tried to "establish positive images of Chinese Americans" by foregrounding cultural differences and ethnic values.[19] The paradoxical truth, however, is that Wong's intention to depict positive images of Chinese Americans inevitably leads her writing to be "restricted and defined by the social acceptance of Chinese Americans."[20] In this regard, Yin acknowledges, "Wong is highly selective in how she portrays Chinese American life and identifies only with elements that are considered characteristics of a model minority."[21] Despite Yin's sympathetic reading, Wong's highlighting of the ethnic differences as if they were *inherent* qualities in Chinese leads the dominant white readers to perceive the Chinese as essentially different cultural others. In this respect, I would rather argue that Wong's ways of seeking acceptance and recognition through promoting ethnic differences contributes to a reinforcing of the socio-cultural hierarchy between the dominant and the marginal, or whites and racial/ethnic minorities.

Unlike Yin's emphasis on Wong's "pioneering role" in Chinese American literature, Karen Su has criticized Wong, especially regarding her political standpoint. Su argues that Wong has "outlived her value as a pioneer and product of her time" and problematizes her politically acquiescent attitude.[22] In fact, in 1953 the U.S. State Department arranged a tour for Wong to speak about her story of success from a female Chinese American perspective, and Jade Snow's story of success was in a way used as a form of international marketing to promote the image of America as a "land of opportunity." Wong has attested that

> In 1953 the State Department sent me on a four-months' grant to speak to a wide variety of audiences, from celebrated artists in Kyoto to restless Indians in Delhi, from students in ceramic classes in Manila to hard-working Chinese immigrants in Rangoon. I was sent because those Asian audiences who had read translations of *Fifth Chinese Daughter* did not believe a female born to poor Chinese immigrants could gain a toehold among prejudiced Americans.[23]

Wong's claim that everybody can make their wish come true depending on individuals' efforts, regardless of their race, gender, and class backgrounds supports the myth of "America." Indeed, Wong has been "interpellated" as a faithful subject to the dominant American society, and her narrative of a "model minority" has been effectively used for other racial minorities to emulate.[24]

Whereas Yin has been positive about Wong's *Fifth Chinese Daughter* in its effort to promote the image of Chinese Americans, Su does not read Wong's narrative of a "model minority" as a product of her time. Rather, she criticizes Wong's politically conservative stance and provides Wong's 1993 convocation speech at Mills College as an example. Su argues that Wong's politically acquiescent attitude embedded in *Fifth Chinese Daughter* is still shown in her speech even after 40 years have passed. In the convocation speech, Wong has said that

> Problems of life are inescapable. Prejudice is only one of them and not the weight of them. There's prejudice against the rich, against the poor, against the young, against the old, against immigrants, against liberals, against the handicapped, against Eskimos, against Indians, and so on. . . . American society, in fact, can be united. . . . Push for equal treatment, but don't whine for preferential treatment.[25]

Su points out that Wong's claim of prejudice being everywhere, and everyone suffers from prejudice, endorses the "neoconservative model of multiculturalism" that attacks "group rights on the principle of equality of individuals."[26] Furthermore, Wong's comments on "preferential treatment" for racial/ethnic minorities—which seems to reflect her own position on affirmative action, a hot issue in the 1990s—mean in essence that Wong reproduces the dominant white American's perspective on affirmative action, even using herself as an example to attest that racism is not a problem. Wong's downplaying of the structural inequality in U.S. society shows that she indeed has internalized the ideology of a "model minority." In this regard, Wong's 1993 speech is an updated version of her 1950s tour sponsored by the State Department.[27]

In fact, the "model minority" narrative, shown through Wong's *Fifth Chinese Daughter,* has actualized the assimilationist success myth by stressing that everybody, regardless of their racial and cultural differences, can achieve his/her dream in the United States by being diligent and by making efforts towards achieving higher education. Although the label "model minority" was created by white Americans, it has been true that many Asian American writers engage in exploiting the stereotype in order to survive or enter mainstream literary markets. In other words, they have tacitly collaborated with the mainstream publishers' demand on minority writers by participating in the reproduction of stereotypical images that dominant groups expect in the media.

In this regard, I would argue that *Fifth Chinese Daughter* obediently fits into the stereotypical image that dominant power groups have projected for Asian Americans. In the book, the narrator Jade Snow says that no obstacles will matter in the accomplishment of her dream, while downplaying inequality and racism apparently at work in society. In the part where Jade Snow depicts her experience as a servant working for an American family, she even shows appreciation for their giving her a chance to become an "intimate" part of them by working for the family: "The Kaisers were kind to Jade Snow and the children never took advantage of her. After her work was done, she enjoyed the new, rare thrill of being able to close her door and be alone within four walls, in peace and quietness."[28] The way Wong depicts her experience as a servant for a white family is rather subservient, as if she were trying to please white American readers, and it also reveals that she is constantly aware of the white-dominated readership and the mainstream literary market's response.

Wong in her autobiography does not question the racist reality whereby equal opportunities have not been given to minorities. Despite Jade Snow receiving a college education after overcoming economic difficulty with her hard work and patience, what she actually faces is a racially discriminating reality, which is contradictory to her own belief in individual success in the United States: "She [Jade Snow] has been told that because she was Chinese, she could not go into equal competition with Caucasians. Her knowledge that racial prejudice existed had never interfered with her personal goals."[29] Avoiding criticism of the inequality and racism working against minorities, Jade Snow tries to overcome the barriers by means of her own efforts, which American society then could hold out as an ideal model for other racial minorities.

The paradoxical truth about the racist reality faced by minorities is ironically revealed, however, when Jade Snow, having failed to get a job even after her college graduation, decides to set up a pottery store in her Chinatown. Although it is a quite pathetic circumstance for her to return to her Chinatown when she had wanted to get out and show her independence from her family, the place she eventually ends up in is her ethnic community. Upon remembering the high grade she received on her writing project about Chinatowns, Jade Snow decides to sell Chinese pottery in her Chinatown. Her decision reflects an acknowledgement of how ethnically different cultural artifacts can become marketable and "exotic" commodities in the white dominant consumer markets. Her pottery business in her Chinatown comes to attract travelers' eyes and later her Chinese pottery business brings her a huge success.

> Strangers turned to stare long and curiously. Caucasians came from far and near to see her work, and Jade Snow sold all the pottery she could make. Even before it had been fired, the first piece was eagerly spoken

for by the man who had kindly found her bricks for the window. But the Chinese did not come to buy one piece from her.

Then those who had laughed hardest stopped. After two months, the mud-stirring maiden was still in business! After three months, she was driving the first postwar automobile in Chinatown. The skeptics knitted their brows. . . . Some Chinese approached the proprietor for information. Was it because her clay came from China? Was it because she had invented a new chemical process to make pottery?[30]

Her success as a minority woman who has overcome poverty and difficulty by her individual efforts ironically reflects that her success became possible by commodifying ethnic/cultural products and by arousing "exotic" appeals. The scene of Jade Snow's baking Chinese pottery becomes a spectacular exhibition in the eyes of visitors. Jade Snow's business within the ethnic boundary of Chinatowns in a way reflects that she has turned her "marginality" itself into a commodity while exoticising culturally distinctive values. Commercial trade in ethnically diverse cultural products has been highlighted in the capitalist market economy, where the difference itself becomes marketable or becomes an exchange value.

However, uneven power relations between minority groups and dominant power groups have always been underlying in commercial transactions of ethnic products. Mainstream literary markets' demand for ethnic autobiography (which allegedly is a "better" form for ethnic writers to deliver their authentic experiences) or for marketing culturally distinctive products as an "authentic" representation of the "exotic otherness" within ethnic boundaries, veils the underlying unequal power relations in society.[31] Just as Jade Snow's Chinese pottery business became successful by spectacularizing the Chinese cultural distinction and caught the attention of the mostly Caucasian visitors to Chinatown, Wong's success from publishing *Fifth Chinese Daughter* becomes possible through her participation in "exoticising" cultural "marginality" for the white-dominant mainstream readers. In this respect, the popularity garnered by Wong from *Fifth Chinese Daughter* leads us to gauge the unequal power relations that infiltrated the production of her book and her politically acquiescent attitudes towards dominant power groups in society.

"ORIENTALS" IN SHOWCASES: AMY TAN'S *THE JOY LUCK CLUB*

In the case of Tan's *The Joy Luck Club*, the idea of turning short stories into a novel did not occur until Sandra Dijkstra, Tan's literary agent, sold the proposal of a collection of her short stories to Putnam. Later the publisher began planning a marketing strategy for the book and urged Tan to finish the novel within a couple of months.[32] The year 1989, when *The Joy Luck Club* was published, was the time of the massacre at Tienanmen Square.[33] It is true that the incident highlighted the problems facing the Chinese government, and external pressures upon the Chinese government to open the door towards the capitalist system have intensified since then.

The Joy Luck Club weaves a story centering around four Chinese women and their American-born daughters, while foregrounding the tragic experience of Suyuan Woo, who left her babies behind in the middle of war-torn China. Just as Ling has mentioned that Chinese Americans were encouraged to describe their personal experiences of the horrors of war with Japan through their writings, the publication of Tan's *The Joy Luck Club* likewise is a faithful response to the mainstream literary market's demand.[34]

Tan's novel implicitly celebrates the journey of Chinese women, migrating full of hope and with the American Dream in their mind. June (Jing-mei) Woo says, "My mother [Suyuan Woo] believed you could be anything you wanted to be in America."[35] Rose Hsu Jordan says, "It was this belief in their *nengkan* (the ability to do anything he put his mind to) that had brought my parents to America."[36] Tan's belief in American society as a "liberating dream country" is depicted through the tale of a woman and a swan.

> The old woman remembered a swan she had bought many years ago in Shanghai for a foolish sum. This bird, boasted the market vendor, was once a duck that stretched its neck in hopes of becoming a goose, and now look!—it is too beautiful to eat. Then the woman and the swan sailed across an ocean many thousands of li wide, stretching their necks toward America. On her journey she cooed to the swan: "In America I will have a daughter just like me. But over there nobody will say her worth is measured by the loudness of her husband's belch. Over there nobody will look down on her, because I will make her speak only perfect American English. And over there she will always be too full to swallow any sorrow! She will know my meaning, because I will give her this swan—a creature that became more than what was hoped for."[37]

The tale of the woman and the swan, which is embedded with dreams and ambitions of immigrant women looking for a better life, in a way represents immigrants' hopes for success and achievement of their American Dream. The central point here is that Tan emphasizes the issue of language. Suyuan Woo wishes her daughter June to speak "only perfect American English." In order to speak perfect American English, immigrants are encouraged to assimilate to the standard and core values of American culture and accommodate themselves to the society's demand. Tan reveals, through the Chinese women's wish, her assimilationist tendency towards the white-dominant society. Her emphasis on individual talents such as language skill as a path of immigrant success supports the myth of a "model minority" and contributes to concealing racial discrimination in the United States. The ideology that Tan reveals is closer to a conservative viewpoint, because conservative multiculturalists argue that racial/cultural minorities should acquire proper language skills in American English and learn the core values of the society before they lay claim to their racial or cultural difference in society. Tan, through her text, speaks for the white bourgeois' belief in America as a country where everyone is treated equally as long as they work hard and have qualified skills. Tan boosts the myth of the American dream and reinforces the stereotypical ideology of Asian Americans as a "model minority."

In *The Joy Luck Club*, Suyuan Woo is the one who initiated a weekly mah-jong game with three other Chinese women. After Suyuan passed away, June, her daughter, recounts the story of her mother, and the stories of other Chinese women in becoming a part of the Joy Luck Club:

> Joy Luck was an idea my mother remembered from the days of her first marriage in Kweilin, before the Japanese came. That's why I think of Joy Luck as her Kweilin story. It was the story she would always tell me when she was bored, when there was nothing to do, when every bowl had been washed and the Formica table had been wiped down twice, when my father sat reading the newspaper and smoking one Pall Mall cigarette after another, a warning not to disturb him. This is when my mother would take out a box of old ski sweaters sent to us by unseen relatives from Vancouver. She would snip the bottom of a sweater and pull out a kinky thread of yarn, anchoring it to a piece of cardboard. And as she began to roll with one sweeping rhythm, she would start her story.[38]

The Chinese women's weekly mah-jong implies that they have found a moment of peace in their new life and they have some time to unravel their past, which in some ways reflects that they have successfully settled down in the United States. The Joy Luck Club thus symbolizes the economic success and leisure they have achieved after they immigrated to the United States: "We were the lucky ones," the Joy Luck Club mothers say.[39] The luck they mention is related to how lucky they feel to have escaped a terrible China and achieved material success in the United States, where they believed that opportunities are open to everyone.

Suyuan Woo, a Kuomintang officer's wife, originally formed the Joy Luck Club in Kweilin in late 1940s as a reminder of the fact that they were still alive despite the Japanese bombing. To Suyuan and the other three Chinese women, the Joy Luck Club meant a symbol of survival and good fortune. Later Suyuan, saved by American missionaries in the middle of war and immigrating to America as a war refugee, reforms her Joy Luck Club in the Chinatown of San Francisco in 1949. The year 1949 signifies the Communist Revolution in China. Tan, through the title of the novel, draws an indirect contrast between pre-Communist China and the China that emerged after 1949, when many Chinese came to the United States as political refugees under an oath of anti-Communism. Whereas the Kweilin Joy Luck Club was formed to celebrate their survival in the middle of war with Japan, the San Francisco Joy Luck Club after their escape to the United States is intended to celebrate material affluence and success in the U.S. capitalist society. The difference in the San Francisco Joy Luck Club is that Joy Luck Club mothers have decided to invest in the stock market with the money they earn from their weekly mah-jong game. The Joy Luck Club members explain that the reason they changed direction is to get an "equal" share of luck: "Now we can all win and lose equally. We can have stock market luck."[40] The Joy Luck uncles also come to the weekly club and the meeting starts by reading the weekly stock exchange:

> Our capital account is $24,825, or about $6,206 a couple, $3,103 per person. We sold Subaru for a loss at six and three-quarters. We bought a hundred shares of Smith International at seven. Our thanks to Lindo and Tin Jong for the goodies. . . . Uncle Jack, who is Auntie Ying's younger brother, is very keen on a company that mines gold in Canada. "It's a great hedge on inflation," he says with authority. He speaks the best English, almost accentless.[41]

The seemingly incidental change in the direction of the San Francisco Joy Luck Club reveals that the Joy Luck Club members follow the path of the majority of people in America in order to gain more profits in a capitalist system. In addition, they emphasize that this is a better way to distribute the profits equally.

In *The Joy Luck Club,* Tan does not mention anything about whether Chinese immigrant women have experienced racism and labor exploitation in the United States or why their lives are still confined in Chinatowns. Instead, the Chinese women's tragic experiences and oppressive Chinese patriarchic cultures are centered around the stories of their American-born daughters, who are already successfully grown up speaking "perfect

American English" as their mothers had wished. The Chinese mothers' wish to make their daughters be like perfect Americans is foregrounded in the beginning of the novel and the Chinese mothers' tragic experiences slip in between their daughters' stories. However, the overall structure of the book is, in my view, based on oppositional binaries between oppressive Chinese culture and free American culture, Communist China and Capitalist America, Chinese immigrant mothers who speak broken English and their American-born Chinese daughters who speak perfect American English. The oppositional relations between the binaries are mainly unfolded around the conflicts between the Chinese mothers and their American-born daughters. The misunderstanding and conflicts between them come to be partially resolved when June visits China to meet her half-sisters, whom Suyuan left behind in the middle of war.

In large part, June's reunification with her half-sisters became possible when China opened the door to the United States and started adapting itself to the capitalist economic system. It has been almost forty years since Suyuan left China in 1949. June, who is now thirty-six years old, represents the accomplishment of Suyuan's wish for her daughter in America. Just as the year 1989, in which *The Joy Luck Club* was published, was the time of China's significant change towards the capitalist system, so is June's visit to China in a way her personal account of the change in China. June is surprised, because what she actually sees is the changed China under the capitalist system, a China that seems totally different from what she has heard about from her mother.

Tan describes the details of how China has changed through June's eyes. June has reserved an inexpensive hotel, but the Garden Hotel in Huanshi Dong Lu looks like a grander vision of the Hyatt Regency:

> Our rooms are next to each other and are identical. The rugs, drapes, bedspreads are all in shades of taupe. There's a color television with remote-control panels built into the lamp table between the two twin beds. The bathroom has marble walls and floors. I find a built-in wet bar with a small refrigerator stocked with Heineken beer, Coke Classic, and Seven-Up, mini-bottles of Johnnie Walker Red, Bacardi rum, and Smirnoff vodka, and packets of M & M's, honey-roasted cashews, and Cadbury chocolate bars. And again I say out loud, "This is communist China?"[42]

Along with June's wondering about China's change towards capitalism, there are June's relatives in China, who want to have "hamburgers, French fries, and apple pie a la mode" for dinner instead of traditional Chinese food, which June has envisioned having in China. "That's what they want," says

June's father implying that Chinese people have more freedom even in the choice of food under a capitalist market economy.[43] Despite June's surprise at her Chinese aunt's response and the fact that she looks somewhat askance at the change of China to capitalism, Tan through June's eye-witness report provides readers with vivid pictures of changing China, and *The Joy Luck Club* indirectly celebrates the change of China to a capitalist system.

Although the intergenerational conflicts between the Chinese immigrant mothers and their American-born daughters comprise a significant part of the narrative, Tan's *The Joy Luck Club* mainly celebrates immigrants' success stories, while putting the extraordinary and painful experience of the Chinese mothers in the center of the novel. Avoiding the treatment of domestic racial issues in her story, Tan instead fills up the space with the tragic stories that Chinese women experienced during the war with Japan and celebrates China's change to capitalism. To my thinking, Tan displays the stories of the Chinese women like "exhibited spectacles" in a showcase drawing readers' attention to their bizarre stories while leaving out specific socio-economic and historical contexts that relate to the mothers' negative experiences in the United States.

The popular recognition accorded to *The Joy Luck Club* by middle-class white American women (who appreciate *The Joy Luck Club*'s portrayals of mother-daughter relations as "universal stories with which they themselves identify"[44]) ironically reveals that Tan mainly satisfies the white-dominated readers' tastes. In fact, Tan has decontextualized the specific socio-economic circumstances of the Chinese women, and she instead has theatricalized the tragic experiences that the Chinese women had undergone. In this respect, Tan has actively participated in selling cultural or ethnic difference as a form of exotic commodity. Patricia Chu points out an ideological tendency that Tan has revealed in her novel as follows: "Tan's novel [*The Joy Luck Club*] lacks historical self-consciousness about the enabling conditions for female self-assertion in America. It naively universalizes its lessons about self-empowerment, disregarding the more serious obstacles to autonomy faced by Chinese women."[45] The Chinese culture in old China, which includes selling girls or exploiting women as a sort of reproductive machine, is patently oppressive and patriarchal. However, the way Tan describes the problematic issues in Chinese culture is rather superficial and they are displayed as sensual and exotic spectacles. In depicting the stories of An-mei Hsu's mother, the fourth wife of a rich man named Wu Tsing, Tan seems to concentrated on exposing tension and jealousy among the wives of Wu Tsing, which might be sensed as bizarre and erotic from the non-Chinese beholders' view. Whereas Suyuan's tragedy, which occurred in the middle of war with Japan, is sympathetically described through June's eyes, the stories of An-mei's mother as a concubine of a rich man are depicted at a certain distance, with an emotionally detached tone, and Tan does not provide readers with the social and economic contexts of how Chinese women's socio-economic status was totally defined by and dependent on men in Chinese patriarchal culture.

The manner in which Tan delivers the stories of four Chinese women seems to be more intended to provide American readers with provocative, consumable, and entertaining cultural stories. In effect, Tan's *The Joy Luck Club* has contributed to commodifying Chinese culture while using her ethnic difference as a strategic marketing tool. To my thinking, *The Joy Luck Club*, Tan's first novel, is an extension of her business writing approach in that she draws attention strategically from readers, while theatricalizing Chinese cultures as "exotic spectacles."[46]

"PERCEIVED EXOTICISM": MAXINE HONG KINGSTON'S *THE WOMAN WARRIOR*

Many minority writers write about their lives in their countries of origin or their lives in the adopted countries in the form of autobiography. Wong's *Fifth Chinese Daughter*, written as a third person narrative, is her autobiographical story, and Kingston's *The Woman Warrior*, although the book is more fictionally woven, has been sold under the category of nonfiction. Autobiography has often been "marketed as unmediated expressions of the lived authenticity of ethnic difference,"[47] and minority writers have been encouraged to deliver their "authentic" experiences and "ethnic" differences through autobiography. E.D. Huntley has noted that autobiography written by minority writers functions more like anthropology in that it explains to Western readers about cultures, rituals, daily life, food, and traditions through personal accounts of life. [48] However, authenticity as depicted through autobiography still remains an issue. For example, early autobiographies and memoirs imprinted American readers with some stereotypical images, according to Huntley, of Chinese houses "furnished with silk carpets and decorated with jade and porcelain artifacts, surrounded by gardens burgeoning with exotic blooms."[49] Autobiography by ethnic writers in some ways reinforced existing stereotypes, and the writers were encouraged to provide the predominantly white readers with "expected" authenticity. Huggan argues that the mainstream literary market's demand for ethnic minorities to write in the form of autobiography could be better understood in the context of a market-oriented view of ethnic differences.

> Ethnic autobiography, like ethnicity itself, flourishes under the watchful eye of the dominant culture; both are caught in the dual processes of commodification and surveillance. This might help explain why the work of writers who come from, or are perceived as coming from, ethnic minority backgrounds continues to be marketed so resolutely for a mainstream reading public as 'autobiographical.'[50]

Huggan points out that cultural difference and "ethnic" authenticity delivered in the form of autobiography have been commodified in late capitalism to the extent that the cultural difference comes to denote "essentially" different "cultural otherness." Publishing companies' market-oriented strategy toward literary works by minority writers has also played an important role in commodifying cultural differences.

If Wong's *Fifth Chinese Daughter* and Tan's *The Joy Luck Club* have received popular recognition by catering to the existing stereotypes of "Orientals," an "exotic," or a "model minority," Kingston's *The Woman Warrior*, which was well received in literary and academic circles, leads us to question whether its popularity is also the consequence of the writer's assimilation to the dominant ideology of the society, while conforming to white readers' expectation of "mythical Orientals." It is known that an editor at Alfred Knopf urged Kingston to publish her book under the category of autobiography. Regarding the "nonfiction" label on the cover of *The Woman Warrior*, Kingston says, "The only correspondence I had with the publisher concerning the classification of my books was that he said that Non-fiction would be the most accurate category; Non-fiction is such a catch-all even poetry is considered non-fiction."[51] Jeffery Paul Chan has criticized Alfred Knopf for having published Kingston's *The Woman Warrior* as "biography rather than fiction" and castigates the autobiographical label as the publisher's "marketing ploy."[52] In addition, Susan Brownmiller, who interviewed Kingston, mentions that the title, *The Woman Warrior: Memoirs of a Girlhood Among Ghosts,* is not Kingston's "first choice" and the title itself is "mildly deceiving" to readers, even before they come to read the book.[53]

Responding to the critics who have misinterpreted her book, Kingston states that she did not want the title to be "The Woman Warrior," which is a fighting image. In fact, Kingston disclosed that the publisher is the one who titled the book, although she herself resists complete identification with the war heroine: "I don't like warriors. I wish I had not had a metaphor of a warrior, a person who uses weapons and goes to war. I guess I always have in my style a doubt about wars as a way of solving things."[54] Despite the image of a warrior woman as a purely artistic strategy, that image became foregrounded by her editor. Publishing companies' marketing strategies have always overridden writers' wishes and have often diverted readers' attention to a certain angle, which might be different from what writers want to convey. Especially in the case of minority writers, the image that editors or publishing companies try to highlight seems to reflect their commercial interests and their stereotypical expectations for literary works by minority writers.

Once *The Woman Warrior* arrived to the public in 1976, the book won an immediate popularity with mainstream white women readers. However, many Asian American critics calumniated Kingston. For instance, Benjamin Tong has criticized Kingston's *The Woman Warrior* by calling it a "fashionably feminist work written with white acceptance in mind."[55] Explaining what she intended to convey through *The Woman Warrior* in her article "Cultural Mis-readings by American Reviewers," Kingston later argues that the critics who favorably reviewed *The Woman Warrior* as an Oriental fantasy "praise the wrong things."[56] Kingston at the same time criticizes some Asian American critics who accused her of "fortifying ethnic stereotypes" through her book. The frustration Kingston had after the publication of *The Woman Warrior* is that, despite her intention to demystify western viewers' Orientalism and their stereotypical view of Chinese, her book is instead perceived as an "exotic Oriental fantasy." Disappointed with readers' stereotypical understandings of her book, Kingston says,

> How stubbornly Americans hang on to the oriental fantasy can be seen in their picking The White Tigers' chapter as their favorite. Readers tell me it ought to have been the climax. But I put it at the beginning to show that the childish myth is past, not the climax we reach for. Also, 'The White Tigers' is not a Chinese myth but one transformed by America, a sort of kung fu movie parody.[57]

In this regard, it is especially useful to note that the Kung Fu television series, broadcast through the 1970s to 1980s, was very popular. The majority of people have regarded the martial metaphor as a "representative icon" of Chinese culture.

Kingston explains that the reason she utilized a warrior image is to debunk Western viewers' stereotypical image of Asians. However, most viewers instead interpreted the chapter "White Tigers" as an embodiment of mystic Orientals or of exotic Chinese culture. In "White Tigers," the narrator's mother teaches her the song of Fa Mu Lan with a hope that her daughter would "grow up like a warrior woman," a worthy family member. However, the story of Fa Mu Lan that the narrator retells through her dream is not same as the original legend of Fa Mu Lan.[58] There are no tales of Fa Mu Lan bearing a child in battle, and there is no baron whom Fa Mu Lan wreaks revenge on.[59] The narrator *reinvents* the Chinese legend and adapts it into her American environment. She wants to fight for her family like a woman warrior, not with a knife but with a pen. She wants to report the racial discrimination her parents and other immigrants have undergone in the United States and the economic hardship they have experienced as immigrants. The narrator has said,

> When urban renewal tore down my parents' laundry and paved over our slum for a parking lot, I only made up gun and knife fantasies and did nothing useful. From the fairy tales, I've learned exactly who the enemy is. I easily recognize them—business-suited in their modern American executive guise,. . . . The reporting is the vengeance— not the beheading, not the gutting, but the words. And I have so many words—chink words and gook words too—that they do not fit on my skin.[60]

Unlike the reader's stereotypical understanding of the woman warrior as an "Oriental fantasy," what Kingston conveys through the narrator is a report on the racial discrimination her family and other Chinese immigrants have experienced and the "crime" that the government officials committed against the economically marginalized and socially excluded immigrants.

Readers' misunderstanding of *The Woman Warrior* was partially caused by the cover design of the 1977 Vintage paperback edition of *The Woman Warrior,* which reproduces the stereotypical image of "Orientals" as mystical and exotic. Sheng-Mei Ma explains how the cover design of *The Woman Warrior,* which was picked by the publisher, has played a role in deceiving readers into anticipating "exotic Oriental" stories in her book. Ma describes the cover design as follows:

> [A] girl with long black hair and slant eyes is encircled by a fiery dragon, a trite marker for the Orient. The woman warrior cannot be visualized except through iconographic clichés. The book cover and promotional literature are, to be sure, the domain of the publisher, over which the author exercises little, if any, control. . . . The cover simplifies and stylizes it. Kingston's best intentions are overshadowed by the popular taste for tropes within the reach of the human mind.[61]

Despite Kingston's using a warrior theme in order to parody the western stereotypes of Asian (or Chinese) culture, popular reception of *The Woman*

Warrior was channeled to satisfy the mainstream reading public's expectation regarding "exotic Oriental" stories. Katheryn Fong, on the other hand, argues that Kingston is responsible if readers failed to read her text as she intended, and says to Kingston: "The problem is that non-Chinese are reading your fiction as true accounts of Chinese and Chinese-American history."[62] However, if readers have read *The Woman Warrior* as Kingston's "authentic" story of her childhood, the blame should go to the publisher, because the publisher's marketing strategy has obscured Kingston's intention in her book by highlighting the image of an "exotic Oriental" girl on the cover and by labeling it as her autobiography.

The reception of Kingston's *The Woman Warrior* by readers and reviewers can be called "perceived exoticism,"[63] because the publisher's strategic foregrounding of the text by means of misrepresentation as an "authentic" depiction of "exotic Orientals" has significantly influenced readers' perception of her book. In other words, critics' accusations against Kingston for arousing exoticism should be differently articulated in that the "exotic" elements that readers read into *The Woman Warrior* are not inherently embedded in her text. Rather, they are the "perceived exoticism" as "marketed and distributed for Western audiences" by the publisher.[64] The heated debates over Kingston's *The Woman Warrior* by this token ironically reflect an "asymmetry in power between 'ethnic minority' writers and the dominant publishing industry," and the "persistence of Orientalism in cultural production and reception."[65] Possible misinterpretation or misunderstanding of literary works by "ethnic" writers is also related to readers' preconceived misconceptions or stereotypes of ethnic writings. What catches beholders' eyes reflects their interests and their ideologies.

I would now like to turn to a discussion of gender issues and immigration problems touched on by this book. In *The Woman Warrior*, Kingston has skillfully woven her text in many layers, while allowing possibilities for multiple interpretations. For instance, "No Name Woman," the first part of *The Woman Warrior*, is replete with cautious warnings. The prohibitive tone ("Don't tell") brings lots of attention to the story. The narrator's father has denied the existence of his sister for her shaming his family with illegitimate pregnancy. The scene of the village people's collective punishment for her illegitimate pregnancy reveals an oppressive aspect of Chinese patriarchal culture. On the other hand, the reason the narrator's mother tells the forbidden story of her aunt to the narrator is to warn her daughter, since she just started menstruation. Regardless of her parents' reason for concealing her aunt from her family, the narrator tries to understand the circumstances affecting her aunt: "She might have separated the rapes from the rest of living if only she did not have to buy her oil from him or gather wood in the same forest."⁶⁶ While imagining her aunt's story within social and economic contexts, the narrator comes to sympathize with her unknown aunt and tries to restore her aunt's erased identity.⁶⁷ It is apparent in the text that Kingston is elucidating the sexually oppressive Chinese patriarchal culture, especially towards Chinese women. The narrator has grown up in a misogynistic environment, listening to phrases such as "Girls are maggots in the rice" or, "It is more profitable to raise geese than daughters." If the narrator's resistance to the oppressive Chinese patriarchal culture has been clearly revealed in the outer layer of her text, there is also an underlying layer that Kingston intends to develop throughout the book.

The mother's message, "Don't tell," is not limited only to the name-less aunt, who had drowned herself in a well. Kingston implicitly connects the social contexts of the aunt's tragic consequence to restrictive U.S. immigration laws, which have prevented Chinese women from migrating to the United States.

> In 1924 just a few days after our village celebrated seventeen hurry-up weddings—to make sure that every young man who went 'out on the road' would responsibly come home—your father and his brothers and your grandfather and his brothers and your aunt's new husband sailed for America, the Gold mountain. . . . Those lucky enough to get contracts waved goodbye from the decks. They fed and guarded the stow-aways and helped them off in Cuba, New York, Bali, Hawaii.⁶⁸

At the outset of the story, Kingston foregrounds the historical and legal backgrounds that conditioned the lives of Chinese men in their journey to the U.S. as contract workers. After the Page Act of 1875, Chinese women were not allowed to enter the U.S. Thus Chinese men left for America leaving their families behind. However, after 1924, which is the year when the Chinese Exclusion Act was issued, the migration of Chinese workers almost stopped and most Chinese men who were already in the U.S. stayed hoping to earn enough money to bring them back to China. What Kingston implies from the beginning of her story is the tragic consequence that results from the legal exclusion of Chinese women and how U.S. immigration policies have influenced immigrants' lives.

In fact, the legal exclusion that Chinese immigrants and their descendents have experienced in the United States is not much different from the situation of the no-name aunt. Like the no-name woman, the identity of Chinese Americans has not been properly recognized in American society, because they have been treated as aliens or as sojourners who are not going to belong to American society. The erased identity—the treatment of the narrator's aunt in her family—is in some ways similar to the way Chinese immigrants have been legally excluded from being a part of America. The reason that the narrator tries to give the no-name woman recognition is to restore her identity, which has been erased by her family and community, just as the identity of the Chinese American has not been properly recognized in the United States.

Failing to notice the historical and legal contexts of her text, which Kingston provides at the outset, most readers actually seem to focus on the unusual tragic event of the narrator's aunt. David Li points out that foregrounding the context in which the no-name aunt was situated is important to understand her circumstances:

> Can we afford to neglect the history of the era in which Kingston stages her narrative, a narrative about marriage and estrangement, deviation and discipline that occurred under the shadow of legislated racism against Asian Americans? While not to advocate a view of literature as social documentation, a historical note could have prepared the uninformed audience for a more meaningful reading. The editors screened out the context of the other chapters, which might otherwise have provided a sense of history. With the benefit of some context, the reader would probably be less likely to make sweeping judgments about "Chinese oppression of women" if she realized that this atrocious scene of gender oppression in China was in part occasioned by the racial exclusion of Asians in America.[69]

If no-name aunt tells one side of the tragic experiences of many Chinese women after their husbands left them behind, the story of the narrator's mother, Brave Orchid, who was advised by her husband to get a medical degree and later join her family in the United States, represents an aspect of Chinese women's reunion with their husbands in America. Conversely, the story of Moon Orchid, Brave Orchid's sister, depicts a fate of the majority of Chinese women who have never reunited with their husbands after they left.

Most readers and critics have failed to notice how the stories of Brave Orchid and Moon Orchid are well connected to Kingston's overall idea of her book. Instead, they mostly have focused on "No Name Woman," "White Tiger," and "A Song for a Barbarian Reed Pipe," putting forward the interpretation that *The Woman Warrior* is about a "Chinese girl's revolt against a sexist Chinese tradition" and her proclamation of being "American." It is true that most critics have not considered the part of Moon Orchid significantly, and the part of Brave Orchid titled "Shaman" (the episodes of Brave

Orchid as a medical student in China) was just interpreted as a story of an "Oriental exorcist."

The seemingly disconnected stories of Brave Orchid and Moon Orchid come to fit into place when we carefully read the context of the immigration law, which has prevented Chinese women from entering the United States. Brave Orchid, who holds a Chinese medical degree in midwifery, was able to come to the United States by virtue of her professional skills. Kingston in *China Men*, which is the companion book of *The Woman Warrior*, provides some background information for Brave Orchid's entry into the United States. Kingston or the narrator's father (who was a poet in China) writes to his wife in China:

> Here's what you have to do if I'm to bring you to America. . . . I will bring you to America on one condition, and that is, you get a Western education. I'll send you money, which you must spend on school, not on food or clothes or jewelry or relatives. Leave the village. Go to Hong Kong or Canton and enroll in a Western scientific school. A science school. Get a degree. Send it to me as evidence you are educated, and I'll send you a ship ticket. And don't go to a school for classical literature. Go to a scientific school run by white people. And when you get your degree, I'll send for you to come here to the United States.[70]

Since it was almost impossible for Chinese women to immigrate to the United States under the Chinese Exclusion Act, which excluded Chinese women, wives, and prostitutes, the proof of a degree was the only way for Chinese women to legally enter the United States without screening before the 1950s.[71]

Although Brave Orchid has spent a couple of years getting her medical degree in order to come to the United States legally, what she actually experienced is another political screening of Chinese immigrants to determine whether they are politically acceptable: "What year did your husband cut his pigtail?"[72] Through the help of a Chinese man on Ellis Island, Brave Orchid could pass the screening and reunite with her husband. Despite her medical degree, however, Brave Orchid could not use her skills in the United States. Her life is confined to a Chinatown in Stockton, working alongside her husband in their laundry. Since they have always felt that they are legally excluded from being American citizens, they have been planning to return. Legal exclusion has influenced the lives of Chinese immigrants as well as their descendents. The overall oppressive feeling that the narrator has experienced in the United States is in some ways related to the oscillating circumstances that most Chinese immigrants have been conditioned to as sojourners.

Moon Orchid, on the other hand, comes from China to visit her husband, who for thirty years never invited her to the United States even after Chinese women received permission in the reformed immigration law of 1952. Moon Orchid's husband married again in the United States and now he has three children. Moon Orchid is afraid of how her husband would respond to her for visiting him without getting his invitation first. She becomes uneasy with her situation and wishing to find a way to take care of herself in the United States, asks her sister if she could find a job. Brave Orchid responds to her:

> You could be a maid in a hotel. . . . A lot of immigrants start that way nowadays. And the maids get to bring home all the leftover soap and the clothes people leave behind. . . . Immigrants also work in the canneries, where it's so noisy it doesn't matter if they speak Chinese or what. The easiest way to find a job, though, is to work in Chinatown. You get twenty-five cents an hour and all your meals if you're working in a restaurant.[73]

Feeling helpless as an uninvited wife, Moon Orchid thinks of giving up the idea of a visit. With Brave Orchid's encouragement, she later decides to see her husband. However, what she hears from her husband after thirty years of long silence is "You weren't supposed to come here. . . . You can't belong."[74] Moon Orchid feels very ashamed to hear this. She becomes mentally ill and later she is carried to a mental asylum.

If "No Name Woman" tells an aspect of Chinese women's tragic fate after Chinese men left their families behind in China, the story of Moon Orchid represents another tragic story of Chinese women who have endured waiting for a long time for their husbands to come back or to invite them to the United States. Each chapter focuses on Chinese women's stories and is implicitly related to the consequence of Chinese men's migration to the United States and the U.S. restrictive immigration law for Chinese immigrants. In her interview, Kingston mentioned that she had intended to have the women's stories (which were later titled *The Woman Warrior*) and the men's stories (later *China Men*) in one volume, but she eventually decided to make the men's stories separately into a "companion volume" to the women's stories, because they seemed to be conflicting with each other.[75] Despite the differences, the reason Kingston regards *China Men* as *The Woman Warrior*'s companion book is well understood within the context that their lives were both conditioned by U.S. immigration laws.

Kingston in her text has repeatedly used the warning message, "Don't tell" (or "You must not tell anyone"). The overall censure that Chinese immigrants experienced when they fell under investigation of communist conspiracy is well depicted in Kingston's text:

> Occasionally the rumor went about the United States immigration authorities had set up headquarters in the San Francisco or Sacramento Chinatown to urge wetbacks and stowaways, anybody here on fake papers, to come to the city and get their files straightened out. The immigrants discussed whether or not to turn themselves in. "We might as well," somebody would say. "Then we'd have our citizenship for real."
>
> "Don't be a fool," somebody else would say. "It's a trap. You go in there saying you want to straighten out your papers, they'll deport you." . . .
>
> "Don't tell," advised my parents. "Don't go to San Francisco until they leave."
>
> Lie to Americans. Tell them you were born during the San Francisco earthquake. Tell them your birth certificate and your parents were burned up in the fire. Don't report crimes; tell them we have no crimes and no poverty. Give a new name every time you get arrested; the ghosts won't recognize you. Pay the new immigrants twenty-five cents an hour and say we have no unemployment. And, of course, tell them we're against Communism.[76]

Through this passage, Kingston shows that she is keenly aware of the political environment in which Chinese immigrants were situated. Most Chinese immigrants have experienced racial discrimination and their lives have been restricted by U.S. immigration laws. Chinese Refugee Policy has allowed Chinese to migrate massively to the United States under the oath of anti-Communism, but for Chinese immigrants the necessity of answering correctly and remaining politically correct in the United States is invisibly related to their life condition. The fear of political screening against Chinese immigrants in the name of communist conspiracy permeated among Chinese immigrants in Chinatowns during the time. Kingston's depiction of the political circumstance in which Chinese immigrants were conditioned reveals her cautious and yet careful awareness of the political environment that ethnic minorities inhabit in the United States.

Then how is it that Kingston's politically keen awareness, embedded in the text of *The Woman Warrior,* has been filtered through critics' eyes without awakening attention, and how has her popularity been mainly credited to her report on oppressive Chinese traditions regarding women or to her telling of another story of "Oriental fantasy"? In spite of its keenness, Kingston's awareness of the socio-economic and political contexts of immigrants' situations has not been well observed by the majority of readers and reviewers. As Wong says, however, "*The Woman Warrior* 'problem' is seen to rest ultimately on the readers, not the author . . . in that authors have little control over how their published works will be read."[77] The question remains whether Kingston's artistic strategy of subversion and reinvention while providing multiple layers of interpretive possibility is also her strategic response towards mainstream literary markets, in which literary and political censorship have invisibly affected the publication of literary works.

THE MEASURED SILENCE

In her article "Can the Subaltern Speak?" Gayatri Spivak points out that the task of "measuring silences" may become important, especially cases where unequal power relations between two groups exist in society.[78] For politically disenfranchised minority groups, speaking for themselves within the boundary of hegemonic ideology needs a cautious and yet conscious strategy. Pierre Machery has indicated that what is important in a work is "what it cannot say." Similarly, what is important in the production of literary works by minorities is the sound of hush that they are cautiously and continuously emitting throughout the text.

Kingston's *The Woman Warrior*, which is permeated with prohibitive tones and warnings, should in this regard be understood as her conscious awareness of being situated at the edge in society. The cautiousness latent in her text denotes Kingston's political awareness of the situation in which marginalized and disenfranchised minorities or immigrants exist in the United States. The silence of the marginalized groups does not mean that there is no "insurgent consciousness," and the political cautiousness embedded in *The Woman Warrior* is Kingston's strategic voice as a "subaltern subject." In this manner, Kingston's *The Woman Warrior* represents a voice of marginalized Asian Americans. In addition, the political cautiousness depicted in *The Woman Warrior* indirectly indicates the current level of U.S. multiculturalism where cultural difference is tolerated as long as exotic stories are provided, but where minority writers are discouraged from foregrounding political and racial tension and inequality at work in society.

Kingston's popularity should be differentiated from that of Wong and Tan, who have garnered popularity by assimilating to the dominant society. Wong and Tan have muted the voice of the disenfranchised minority by actively interpellating to the mainstream literary markets' demand and by conforming themselves to the dominant power structure and ideology. They have internalized the ideological stereotype of Asian Americans as a "model minority" or an "exotic" through their writings, which eventually helped them to achieve recognition as "successful" ethnic minority writers. Although they have received wide recognition from the majority reading public in the United States, their political acquiescence to the dominant power structure of the society has led them to commodify cultural differences to the point that cultural minorities are exhibited as "exotic others" in the name of cultural diversity.

Although Wong and Tan achieved "popularity" and financial "success" through publication of *Fifth Chinese Daughter* and *The Joy Luck Club,* the exoticized and essentialized cultural differences depicted in their writings ironically prove that they have failed to situate the texts beyond ethnicity. In their ethnic-based approaches they have missed grounding their narrative in the specific socioeconomic, political, and legal contexts to which Asian immigrants were conditioned. Instead, Wong and Tan's politically acquiescent stance with respect to the dominant U.S. culture and politics has led them to merely repeat an already ideologically-woven narrative through their stories, while concealing the unequal power structure and exploitation of labor against racial minorities.

Fifth Chinese Daughter and *The Joy Luck Club* are thus a mere minority literature in that they have participated in reproducing the stereotypes expected by the white majority. The stories of immigrant success based on meritocracy and cultural characteristics portrayed in Wong's and Tan's texts have helped to conceal the unequal power relations in society and have limited the possibility of reading beyond ethnicity in U.S. multicultural literary works. Although Wong and Tan have garnered financial success, their "popularity" does not carry with it any reputation as representative Asian American writers, in the sense of consciously trying to reflect through their writings the social and economic contexts in which Asian immigrants were situated. In this regard, the politically silent voice and acquiescence embedded in Wong's and Tan's writings rather correspond to institutionalized U.S. multiculturalism, which advertises the image of "America" as a "land of opportunity." Just as the stereotype of Asian Americans as a "model minority" has helped to conceal the unequal power structure and racism at work in society, so have politically acquiescent multicultural writings, as represented in Wong's and Tan's texts, contributed towards sustaining the U.S. power structure in the name of the particular form of cultural diversity promoted by U.S. multiculturalism.

Politically Conscious Asian American Multiculturalism

The rebellious voices that politically conscious multiculturalists—whether they are writers, critics, activists, or critical minorities/immigrants—sound through their writings have not been properly received and appreciated in U.S. society or the mainstream literature market. The dissident voice sustained by politically conscious multiculturalism delineates a critical distance from dominant American culture and politics. It is an expression of disagreement with the U.S. political and economic policy toward other worlds as well as an angry reaction against inconsistent and ambivalent attitudes and policies affecting minorities and immigrants within the nation.

In a departure from the celebration of immigrants' success stories, which are mostly silent about the political and economic conditions that have brought people to the United States and are amenable to the U.S. dominant ideology, my goal is to reveal—with a dissident voice—how cheap, colonized immigrant labor has been economically and ideologically exploited in the process of U.S. capital formation; how the United States has managed the political, economic, and ideological crisis produced by such exploitation; how the issues of U.S.-centered globalization and differentiation of immigrants within the nation are interconnected. In effect, I hope to clarify my sense that the United States has established and maintained a hegemony and Empire.

To contextualize my discussion, I will address some Marxist theories of capitalist development as well as the current theoretical debate about globalization. Although I will largely be drawing on the critical theory of capitalist expansionism, the political, legal, and ideological elements that lead to the vulnerable status of immigrants in the United States will be treated in reference a variety of theories.

The United States has expanded its power or accumulated its capital through military interventions and involvement in various wars, through the migration of capital to other worlds, or through economic sanctions using the International Monetary Fund (IMF) and World Bank. It is not my intention to totalize the world economy, politics, or the phenomenon of immigration in general. By contextualizing the historical, political, and economic elements that have influenced the production of multicultural literary texts, I shall be attentive to the narratives of immigrants whose lives to such an extent have been shaped by the historical or economic conditions of the ongoing global restructuring of the world. For example, Yamashita's *Tropic of Orange* criticizes how the inequitable North American Free Trade Agreement (NAFTA) policies have been used to enable U.S. capitalists to penetrate other countries for U.S. commodity markets. Ozeki's *My Year of Meats* interrogates the U.S.-centered violent restructuring of the global economy by means of the interpenetration of giant corporations and by means of media imperialism. Bulosan's *America Is In the Heart* speaks from the collective experience of Filipinos—whose nation has been colonized by the U.S.; who have been dispossessed from their land by absentee landlords; whose massive migration to the United States has dislocated them from the family; whose colonized body has been economically exploited as cheap labor and ideologically used for building racial tension in order to stabilize the nation in economic, political, and ideological terms—and needs to be thoroughly understood in the context of the U.S. colonialism, neocolonialism, and global capitalization.

Marxist philosophy and analysis cannot fully provide an explanation for the political, economic, and ideological management of capitalist crisis within the U.S. borders. This has been well explained in Lisa Lowe's post/ neo-colonial reading of the current phenomenon of migration, especially to the United States. Lowe determines that Asian migration, especially since 1965, is closely related to the U.S. neocolonization of the Asian countries (such as Vietnam, Laos, Cambodia, Taiwan, the Philippines, and South Korea). She interprets the Asian immigration to the United States as the "return to the imperial center."[1] Lowe's postcolonial reading of migration and the "gendered racialization" of Asian immigrants (which is another form of domestic colonization of immigrant bodies) gives an insight into the racialized/colonized labor force in the United States. Lowe's analysis of the migration to the United States from the countries where the U.S. influence was dominant allows us to understand the phenomenon of immigration in its connection to U.S. expansionism and how the immigrants, as the invisible U.S. colonized bodies, serve to sustain the U.S. Empire. Lowe's analysis of Asian migration as a consequence of U.S. neo-colonization and the role of immigration law as an "oppressive apparatus" fills a major gap, since Marxist analysis cannot provide an explanation of how the specific histories of U.S. neocolonization and imperialism have displaced the people from their origin, which leads the invisibly colonized to become "racialized" in the domestic labor force.

However, Lowe's analysis also reveals limitations in the understanding of the phenomenon of migration, which is international. Although I agree with Lowe's analysis of the phenomenon of Asian migration as the "return to the imperial center" and the use of immigrant labor as cheap, domestic "colonized" bodies, I have some concern regarding her explanation of Marxist analysis as a "universal" theory, which "cannot account for the current global restructuring of capitalism in which U.S. capital maximizes its profits through strategies of 'mixed production' and 'flexible accumulation' that cross national boundaries."[2] Lowe's criticism of Marxist theory, in my view, seems to reveal a limited understanding of Marxism. In effect, Marxists/neo-Marxists argue that the tendency of capitalist expansionism is to search not only for "new markets and raw material," but for "new sources of accumulation" from the employment of labor: "Capital invested in colonies, etc., may yield a higher rate of profit for the simple reason that the rate of profit is higher there on account of the backward development, and for the added reason that slaves, coolies, etc. permit a better exploitation of labour."[3] To my thinking, the Marxist theory of creating surplus value is not contradictory to Lowe's argument of accumulating profit through the "differentiation of specific resources and markets that permits the exploitation of gendered and racialized labor within regional and national sites."[4]

In understanding why the United States uses immigrants as cheap labor sources, there seems to be a difference between Marxist reading and Lowe's post/neocolonial reading of the phenomenon of migration. Whereas Marxist theory understands the phenomenon as a part of the intrinsic logic of capitalist expansionism, which is universal, Lowe's account for the "racialized" Asian immigrants within the U.S. economy gives a specific explanation of the phenomenon. It is right to say that migration of labor is occurring everywhere in the world, especially from the underdeveloped countries to the developed capitalist countries, as Marxist theory argues. Even among Asian countries, migration of labor from Bangladesh, the Philippines, India, and Pakistan to Japan has been occurring. Yet, it is also true that the dominant stream of migration toward the United States is connected to the U.S. cultural, political, and economic influence on the countries, as Lowe argues. I find useful explanations in both readings of the phenomenon of migration. In other words, I would rather argue that we do not need to exclude one theory in order to apply the other. If the dominant element or determinant that either theory or reading provides is caused by its theoretical justification, then the globalized reality, which is complicated and multiply determined by various elements, can be more properly understood when we flexibly apply both theories without excluding one from the other.

Part of my intention in this project is to bring attention to the need for a critical voice that confronts the manner in which the system of oppression has justified the exploitation of racial/ethnic minorities for the system's sake. By contextualizing the historical, political, and economic elements that have influenced the production of multicultural literary texts, I am seeking to foreground the narratives of immigrants, mainly Asians, whose lives have been determined by the historical or economic condition of the ongoing global restructuring of the world as well as by restrictive immigration policies.

The dissident voice that politically conscious Asian American multicultural writings embody is the consequence of U.S. imperialist influence on other worlds. The oppositional position that politically conscious multicultural writers take through their writings is a way of confronting the dominant U.S. politics within and outside the nation. Their dissident voices are not only interrogating U.S.-centered capitalist expansion and the social, political, and economic mechanisms that have scapegoated immigrants in the United States; they are also defiantly confronting dominant literary streams, which have systematically neglected the oppositional position posed by politically conscious multiculturalism. By challenging the conservative and politically acquiescent multiculturalism that continues to reinforce or contribute to the U.S. dominant ideology and its structure, my project will demand that a space be allowed for critical and diverse voices to be recognized.

My goal in Part II is to draw attention to politically conscious Asian American multicultural writings that have been relatively marginalized in the discussion of multicultural literature. In the course of celebrating the immigrants' success stories, which are mostly imbedded in "popular" multicultural literature, the voices of dissidence and distance from the dominant American culture and politics have received little attention from readers and literary markets. For example, John Okada's *No-No Boy* was not hospitably received by either the American or the Japanese community when it was published in 1957. Just as the entire incident of Japanese internment and the issue of draft resistance was buried in the Japanese community, the novel was rejected by both Japanese/Japanese American and American readers, and it took twenty more years for the novel to achieve an academic imprimatur. In a similar vein, *America Is In the Heart* by Carlos

Bulosan was erased from literary history until the late 1970s, and Bulosan's name, in spite of his publications of numerous short stories in magazines and journals, was blacklisted in the 1950s.[5] Most of his works have been overlooked or dismissed from mainstream literary discussions. *America Is In the Heart* depicts the resistance voice of the doubly disenfranchised Filipinos—colonized bodies and a cheap "disposable" labor force—and is an example of a politically conscious multicultural text. As an outsider within the border, the journey that Bulosan has illustrated in his novel urges me to provide a space for a subject like Bulosan, a critical writer/resistant immigrant fighting back against the oppressive mechanism that has exploited and legally bound immigrants or minorities in the United States.

The novels by Carlos Bulosan, Fae Myenne Ng, Karen Tei Yamashita, and Ruth Ozeki, which I categorize as politically conscious multicultural texts, incorporate the issues of U.S.-centered globalization and the exploitation of immigrants under U.S. capitalism. As the first immigrant generation or the descendents of immigrants, the writers—Bulosan, Ng, Yamashita, and Ozeki—maintain their dissident voices and lead us to look at the issues of multiculturalism in the global context while reminding us to consciously react to the racially discriminating American reality.

Chapter Three

Beyond Ethnicity: The Critical Movement in Asian American Literature

An ethnically different group is essential to the society: it is an exploited class supporting the entire edifice.

—Edna Bonacich

Part of my intention in this chapter is to read racially and nationally oppressed Asian immigrants in correlation with historical, legal, and economic circumstances into which minority groups were positioned in the United States during the twentieth century. To my thinking, this analysis is essential, because of academic cultural tendencies to examine multi-ethnic and racial relations solely in cultural contexts, which effaces all recognition that U.S. multiculturalism is a historical consequence that resulted from U.S. economic expansionism and the labor migration of various racial/ ethnic and national groups to the United States.

U.S. multiculturalism's ethnicity-based approach to society in fact diverts racial and class problems and it does not provide a reflection of unequal power relations in society. For instance, if Chinese and Japanese Americans excel at school and move up to middle-class status, their success according to this approach might be attributed to their own cultural assets. Then, the poverty of the majority of other minority groups in this framework will be explained in terms of their cultural inability to improve themselves. Conceivably, the ethnicity-based approach emphasizes that different cultural and ethnical characteristics determine the success and failure of immigrants, at the same time concealing the structural inequality imposed on immigrants in the United States.

What I want to emphasize is that no matter what cultural differences exist among ethnic minorities, socioeconomic and legal discriminations experienced by most Asian immigrants in the United States cannot be solely understood in cultural contexts. Ideological and economic mechanisms as well as legal restrictions that have disenfranchised and oppressed Asian immigrants and other racial/ethnic minorities in the U.S. can be better appreciated when the spectrum of multiculturalism becomes broader and goes beyond the limited scope of ethnicity. The economic, ideological, and legal elements that have influenced the lives of Asian immigrants must be apprehended within the complex interrelations of race, ethnicity, gender, and class in U.S. society. I am seeking to expand the definition of U.S. multiculturalism beyond its academic focus on ethnicity and cultural pluralism and to broaden perspectives of multiculturalism by exploring the socioeconomic and political circumstances faced by racial minorities who have been situated within U.S. capitalist social formation.

Although U.S. multiculturalism's emphasis on cultural difference and diversity is a response to the change in racial/ethnic composition in U.S. society, the change did not merely occur as a result of different racial/ethnic groups' migration to the United States. The underlying reason for the United States becoming more multicultural is closely related to the development of U.S. capitalism.[1] Capitalists' search for cheaper sources of labor power is an inherent logic in the capitalist system, and capitalists' exploitation of the colonized or racial minority workers became an alternative solution to the conflicts occurring between capital and labor. The migration of labor from Asia or other countries was, in effect, a structural consequence of U.S. global expansion and U.S. capitalism. "America" as a multiethnic and multiracial nation was systematically created by capitalists' demands for a cheap labor force in the developmental process of U.S. capitalism.

Moreover, wage differentiations and labor divisions along race/ethnicity lines have been effectively utilized against minority workers, and the differentiation along race and ethnicity lines not only has contributed to the cheapening of minority workers' wages, it has also caused conflicts between domestic workers and racial/ethnic minority workers. The fact that cheap racial minorities were available in domestic labor markets aroused a fear of losing jobs among domestic workers, and anti-immigrant sentiments became a social and economic factor. In other words, the "class antagonism," as Bonacich emphasizes, has taken the "form of ethnic antagonism."[2]

In the case of Chinese and Filipino immigrants, the recruited workers were predominantly males and they suffered from unfair labor contracting and harsh exclusion movements.[3] Chinese workers' forced formation of their own ethnic enclaves is in effect an aspect of harsh racial discrimination and economic exclusion of minority workers. In the case of Filipino workers, the massive migration of Filipinos formed the reserve army of labor in domestic labor markets. The classic conflict with domestic workers flared up sharply during the economic depression of the 1930s. Filipino immigrants were eventually excluded through the passage of the Tydings-McDuffie Act of 1934. The pattern of labor recruitment and exclusion from the society has been repeated throughout U.S. labor history and it reflects the conflicts between capital and labor in U.S. capitalist society, and how racial/ethnic minorities have been ideologically and economically utilized for the system's sake.

In the literary representation of the political and economic circumstances involving labor migration, Bulosan's *America Is In the Heart* portrays how U.S. capitalists have stratified the labor force according to racial and national differences and have justified the exploitation of politically and economically oppressed immigrants as a cheap labor. Ng's *Bone*, set in Chinatown, develops the historical background of the formation of ethnic enclaves, a consequence of socioeconomic and ideological tension occurring between domestic workers and racial minorities in the 1880s. Situating the issues of race and ethnicity in the interactions of gender, class, and nation, Bulosan and Ng use narrative fiction to highlight the specific historical, political, economic, and legal contexts that have conditioned the lives of Asian immigrants. Both writers focus on how Asian immigrants have been politically, economically and ideologically used in domestic labor markets, and they interrogate social and economic mechanisms and restrictive legal policies practiced against Asian immigrants in the United States.

Although Bulosan (a Filipino immigrant) and Ng (a Chinese American) have different national backgrounds, I place them in the same discussion in order to focus on the socioeconomic exploitation and legal exclusions that most Asian immigrants have received in U.S. labor markets. It is also my attempt to go beyond the ethnicity-based approach in reading Asian American multicultural texts. Although *America Is In The Heart* sets its background in the pre-World War II period, the phenomenon of labor migration from the U.S. colonies is still in motion, as the current massive Puerto Rican migration to mainland United States reveals. Ng's *Bone*, despite its setting in the 1990s' San Francisco Chinatown, shows a significant connection between the past and the present of the social and economic situation of Chinese immigrants. Portraying an ongoing restructuring of Chinatown through the depiction of a tragic incident and of hardworking seamstresses at Chinatown sweatshops, Ng indirectly questions whether there is any significant change in the socially and economically marginalized Chinese immigrants from nineteenth-century coolies to Chinatown seamstresses in the 90s.

Combining Bulosan's and Ng's texts in a discussion is, in a sense, to question whether the social and economic status of Asian immigrants has significantly improved despite the media's portrayal of Asian immigrants as a "successful" minority. Although the ideology of Asian Americans as a "docile" and "self-serving model minority" has prevailed since the 1960s, and although many Asian Americans have settled down as middle-class citizens, large numbers of Asian immigrants are still struggling with poverty and living in socially and economically confined ethnic communities. In fact, the problem of the poverty of these immigrants has been underrepresented in the context of Asian immigrants' perceived "success." Asian immigrants still constitute socially excluded and politically silent groups in the United States, as several politically conscious writers have attempted to reveal.

THE COLONIZED AS THE RESERVE ARMY OF LABOR: CARLOS BULOSAN'S *AMERICA IS IN THE HEART*

Carlos Bulosan in *America Is In The Heart* (1946) highlights the conflict between capital and labor occurring in the developmental process of U.S. capitalism and reveals his critical awareness of how Filipino immigrants and other racial minority workers have been politically, economically, and ideologically exploited in U.S. labor markets. Through the title of the book, Bulosan ironically discloses that "American" ideals have not been fulfilled, because American reality is still replete with inequality and exploitation of the labor of racial minorities. Revealing the unrealized "ideal" of "America" and seeking to close the gap between the racially discriminating reality and the ideal principle of the country, Bulosan in *America* questions what "America" means to racial/ethnic minorities or the nationally oppressed in the United States.

The personal/historical stories of this work portray the time when the social and economic problems in the Philippines come bursting out after the multiple colonization by Spain (1565–1898) and the United States (1902–1946). Subtitling the book *A Personal History,* Bulosan weaves the stories from his own experiences as well as those of other Filipinos and emphasizes the Philippines' historical circumstances and the inevitability of Filipino migration. He indicates how the intervention of powerful countries in the Philippines brought a cultural, social, and economic disaster to the indigenous culture and society and eventually led the uprooting of Filipinos and their drift to the United States. Bulosan describes a radical socioeconomic and political change that takes place after U.S. colonization of the Philippines.

All over the archipelago the younger generation was stirring and adapting new attitudes. And although for years the agitation for national independence had been growing, the government was actually in the hands of powerful native leaders. It was such a juicy issue that obscure men with ample education exploited it to their own advantage, thus slowly but inevitably plunging the nation into a great economic catastrophe that tore the islands from their roots, and obfuscated the people's resurgence toward a broad national unity.[4]

He discloses in this passage the social, political, and economic impact of U.S. colonization as well as the deep economic gap between the Philippine landlords (or middle class) and the majority of Filipino peasants and their different political perspectives on the issue of national independence. Bulosan implies a conspiracy between U.S. colonizers and both the Philippine landlords and the middlemen who try to take advantage of the colonial trade-pattern.

So-called absentee landlordism, which has its origin in the Spanish colonization of the Philippines, becomes the main cause of the enslaving and uprooting of the Filipino peasantry, leading the Filipino peasants to struggle against Spain and U.S. colonizers as well as the Philippine landowners. Bulosan expresses how violently the Filipino peasantry, family, and homeland were disrupted by absentee landlordism. Even after the United States replaces the Spanish colonization, landlordism is retained and the feudal agrarian economy is perpetuated. The Philippines' economic dependency on the U.S. thereby becomes unavoidable. In other words, the effect of the Philippines' colonization by Spain and then by the United States is to leave the majority of Filipinos hopeless and miserable in their homeland. Further, the colonial trade relationship makes the Philippines into a market for U.S. manufactured products and this retards the growth of Philippine industry.

In *America* Bulosan focuses on the historical moment when Filipino peasants in the hands of U.S. colonizers are being destroyed at the roots.

One summer day, when the rice lay golden in the sun, startling rumors came to Mangusmana: the peasants in a province to the south of us had revolted against their landlords. . . . They began to think for themselves and to take matters into their own hands, and they resorted to anarchistic methods. But there came a time when an intelligent campaign for revolt was started, with the positive influences of peasant revolts in other lands; and the Philippine peasants came out with their demands, ready to destroy every force that had taken from them their inherited lands.

The unorganized revolt in the southern province ended in tragedy;
the peasants were shot down and those who survived were thrown into
medieval dungeons. But these conditions could not go on for long without disastrously rocking the very foundation of Philippine life. These
sporadic revolts and uprisings unquestionably indicated the malignant
cancer that was eating away the nation's future security and negatively
influencing the growth of the Philippines from a backward and unde-
veloped agricultural land into a gigantic industrial country. The wealth
that was not already in the power of the large corporations, banks, and
the church, was beginning to flow into the vaults of new corporations,
banks, and other groups. As bloodily as this wealth concentrated into
the hands of the new companies, as swiftly did the peasants and workers become poorer.[5]

The news about how U.S. colonizers violently killed the revolting Filipino
peasants and guerillas has spread throughout the islands, and the Filipinos'
animosity towards the U.S. colonizers becomes severe. As a means of releas-
ing tension between native Filipinos and the colonizers as well as to have
Filipinos conform to the purpose of U.S. colonization, the United States
introduces the American education system into the Philippines.

Bulosan depicts how the U.S. educational system has ideologically
uprooted the Filipino young generation and has prepared young Filipinos
for migrating to the United States, the "land of opportunity." Bulosan's
America is in a way an ideological critique of U.S. colonial education, which
has imbued Filipinos with the illusion of "America." In fact, the introduction of U.S. education can be interpreted as an instrument of colonial control, and the U.S. educational system serves as an ideological apparatus
shaping Filipinos' mind and culture. Whereas territorial occupation of the
Philippines established hegemonic power over the Philippines' politics and
economy, the education system established "cultural hegemony" over the
population.[6]

Bulosan centralizes his concern about the U.S. educational system in
the characterization of Allos's brother, Macario. Through the "Americanized" education, the young Filipino generation that received the "Americanized" education has become a faithful "ward" of the colonizers. Allos's
brother Macario manifests a change of attitude after studying in the U.S.
education system. Bulosan represents Macario's transformation in interesting and subtle ways that nonetheless reveal the stark cultural changes
Macario's behavior indicates. When Macario meets his father, he would
rather shake hands with his father instead of kissing his hand, the traditional way of greeting and of showing respect to the older generation. Also

Macario's opinion on Allos's long hair reveals indirectly the change of his way of thinking.

> "Well, let us go home and I will cut your long hair," said Macario to me.
> "Don't you ever cut your hair, brother?"
> I was speechless. I was ashamed to say anything.
> "He needs it for protection against vicious mosquitoes and flies," said my father. "It is also his shield from the sun in hot summer."
> "I will make a gentleman out of him," Macario said. "Wouldn't you like to be a gentleman, Allos?[7]

Macario's response on the subject of Allos's long hair reflects the greater value he places on America's "western" civilization and modernization. The U.S. education system, which is administered from Americans' perspectives, has put the indigenous Filipino culture into an inferior and uncivilized position, and it actually has led Filipinos to internalize the ideologies that might work against the indigenous culture of the Philippines.

The change in Macario's way of thinking towards Filipino culture indirectly reveals how the hierarchical power relationship between the U.S. and the Philippines has infiltrated into the Filipino mind as a result of U.S. education. Filipinos who received U.S. education have slowly adopted "American" customs and civilization-oriented thinking, and they unconsciously, as Macario has shown, put their native culture beneath "American" culture. In this regard, Carey McWilliams argues that U.S. education was successful in educating many young Filipinos away from the islands toward the United States.[8]

Bulosan criticizes the structural control of labor in addition to ideological transformation. The colonial trade pattern between the U.S. and the Philippines, which has notably retarded the growth of Philippine industry, became another contributing factor in city workers being left low waged and unemployed. Thus, the migration of Filipinos to the United States was in a sense unavoidable. In *America*, Allos's decision to come to the United States reflects the Philippines' social and economic circumstances, where families and the peasantry in general are uprooted through absentee landlordism, and where workers are exploited with low wages and suffer from unemployment due to the over-flooding of U.S. manufactured goods in the colonial free-trade relationship.[9] Allos explains the reason for his escape from the Philippines:

> I was getting restless and fearful of the uncertainty that pervaded our household. I felt like running away—anywhere. I wanted to cast off the

sudden gloom that shadowed our family, and I thought the only way to do that was to escape from it. I would also be escaping from my family, and from the bitter memories of childhood.

"I am leaving now, Father," I said one day.

My father said nothing. He simply looked at me. He was trying hard to hold back the tears that were gathering in his eyes. He was remembering and looking through me into the uncertain future and the dark fate that awaited me there, and his mouth trembled a little because he knew what it was I was forsaking, what I was plunging so desperately.[10]

There is little doubt that the push-effect has been generated through colonization. In addition, the U.S. education system in the Philippines, which taught Filipinos that the United States is the ideal place embodying democracy and equality, has augmented the pushing force leading to Filipino migration to the United States.

In this regard, Bulosan's *America* is a representation of Filipinos' lives intertwined with the historical turmoil of the Philippines and its colonization by the United States. *America* is Bulosan's vivid depiction of the unavoidable migration of Filipinos, who are politically, economically, and ideologically dominated by the United States. Since the United States has colonized the Philippines, Filipinos have been classified as U.S. nationals, hence they were allowed to come to the United States without limitation. However, Filipinos were not allowed to apply for U.S. citizenship, because they were not whites; nor were they regarded as aliens, because they were U.S. nationals. This ambiguous status of Filipino identity becomes a target to be exploited in U.S. labor markets. After Allos has arrived in Seattle, he finds that Filipinos are not equally treated as he has learned through the U.S. education. In December 1937, Bulosan writes in his letter: "Western people were brought up to regard Orientals or colored people as inferior, but the mockery of it all is that Filipinos are taught to regard Americans as our equals. . . . The terrible truth in America shatters the Filipino's dream of fraternity."[11]

What Allos faces in the United States is far different from his expectation of "America" as an ideal place. Being sold by a hotel proprietor for five dollars to work in the fish canneries in Alaska, Allos comes to realize that justice and tolerance have not applied to racial/ethnic minorities in the United States. In his essay entitled, "My Education," Bulosan writes: "My departure from the Philippines was actually the breaking of my ground, the tearing up of my roots. As I stayed longer and searched further, this feeling of not belonging became more acute, until it distorted my early vision of America."[12] In *America*, Allos also finds that his brothers call him Carlos, his Christian name, after he has arrived in the United States. Allos's feeling of uprootedness from his homeland and native culture is indirectly revealed through his changed name.

Although the causes of Filipino migration to the United States can be interpreted as a combination of U.S. political, economic, and cultural domination of the Philippines, U.S. demand for cheap labor has been a pull factor that inevitably led Filipinos to migrate to the United States. Filipino workers have been exploited as cheap exchange labor in the United States, which reflects the unequal power relation between the colonizer and the colonized. In other words, the hierarchical relationship between the United States and the Philippines is in conflict with what "Americans" have taught Filipinos through the U.S. education system in the Philippines. Allos/Carlos feels that he is being treated like a cheap "commodity" in U.S. labor markets. Cheng and Bonacich in this regard point out that the migration of people to the United States from the countries under U.S. domination is historically and systematically connected with the dynamics of capitalism because "the displacement of colonized peoples and the requirement of more labor in the capitalist economy arise out of the logic of capitalist development."[13]

From U.S. capitalists' perspective, Filipinos could be used as cheap exchange labor and became a source for the cheap labor supply. Filipinos' massive migration to the United States as cheap labor in fact fulfilled the role of what has been called a "reserve army of labor" by providing a relative surplus population with respect to the domestic labor pool.[14] The recruited Filipino workers were effectively used as a source of cheap labor in domestic labor markets after the Chinese Exclusion law prevented the Chinese from migrating to the United States. The ambiguous status of the Filipino identity made it easier for employers to utilize Filipino laborers in racially, ethnically, and nationally divided domestic labor markets.

In *America,* Bulosan through Allos/Carlos depicts how recruited Filipino workers (or Pinoy, which is a term generally applied to all Filipino immigrant workers) were deceived from the moment they arrived in the United States and were forced to work in unfair conditions:

> We were forced to sign a paper which stated that each of us owed the contractor twenty dollars for bedding and another twenty for luxuries. What the luxuries were, I have never found out. The contractor turned out to be a tall, heavy-set, dark Filipino. . . . They [contractors] had henchmen in every cannery who saw to it that every attempt at unionization was frustrated and the instigators of the idea punished. The companies also had their share in the exploitation; our bunkhouses were unfit for human habitation. The lighting system was bad and dangerous to

our eyes, and those of us who were working in the semi-darkness were severely affected by the strong ammonia from the machinery.[15]

Whereas the political hierarchy between the United States and the Philippines caused a double disenfranchisement of Filipinos in U.S. labor markets, the contracting system, which obscured the hierarchical relationship between direct employers and laborers, has made the situation of Filipinos even worse.[16] Contractors, who mostly consisted of immigrants, have played a role of middlemen between employers and workers. They became an immediate oppressor of workers, overexploiting minority labor in order to have a greater share for their interests.

Bulosan emphasizes the disparity between the ideology of free labor and its actual implementation in labor practices in operation with immigrants. Filipino workers have been utilized as a cheap exchange labor, and the asymmetrical power relationship between the U.S. and the Philippines was effectively used to cheapen wages of Filipino workers. As mentioned earlier, the recruitment of young males contributes to maximizing the surplus to employers. U.S. employers preferred to hire Filipino workers because they were single men and could be housed inexpensively. The working and living conditions in the farm field were unsanitary and undesirable. In *America,* Bulosan through Allos/Carlos describes poor working conditions:

> It was autumn, the season for planting cauliflower. I went to the field at six in the morning and worked until six in the afternoon. It was tiresome, back-breaking work. I followed a wagon that carried cauliflower seedlings. The driver stopped now and then to drop a handful of the seedlings between the long furrows. I picked up the seedlings with one hand and dug into the ground with the other; then, putting a seedling into the hole, I moved on and dug another hole. I could hardly move when six o'clock came. I climbed into the wagon that took me slowly to the town.
>
> The bunkhouse was made of old pieces of wood, and was crowded with men. There was no sewage disposal. When I ate swarms of flies fought over my plate. My bed was a makeshift tent under a huge water tank, away from the bunkhouse. I slept on a dirty cot: the blanket was never washed. The dining room was a pigsty. The cook had a harelip and his eyes were always bloodshot and watery.[17]

Allos/Carlos's experience as Pinoy in U.S. labor markets leads him to realize that Filipinos in the United States are not equally treated, despite what he had learned in the Philippines. What Allos/Carlos experiences is far different from his expectation of "America" as an ideal place where justice and tolerance are equally applied to racial minorities.

Bulosan works to reveal the extent to which employers have tactically split laborers according to race and ethnicity. He writes: "Japanese workers were also arriving from San Francisco, but they were housed in another section of the farm. I did not discover until some years afterward that this tactic was the only way in which the farmers could forestall any possible alliance between the Filipinos and the Japanese."[18] Whereas the labor and wage difference was split along race lines, further stratification among minorities was made along ethnic lines, and each ethnic group was divided from other ethnic groups by contractors as a way to strategically disintegrate the labor organization among minority workers. Although employers could use laborers consisting of a single national group, they preferred to hire people who were different in language, culture, and nation. The reason employers recruited laborers from various racial/national groups was to divide and stratify minority workers by putting barriers among them, which eventually helps to prevent laborers from organizing labor unions. Contractors also played a peculiar role in disintegrating the alliance among minority workers. A strategy of "split labor market" along race lines has been utilized as a way to cheapen the wage of minority laborers and it became the main reason that domestic workers felt threatened.[19]

In addition, negative stereotypes of racial/ethnic immigrants have been conveniently utilized to exploit the labor of racial/ethnic minorities at cheap wage. Although Allos/Carlos has suffered with back-breaking pain and itch from field work, mass media and farm employers have spread the ideologies that Filipinos are "ideal for stoop work." For instance, Frank Waterman of the State Employment Agency told an interviewer in 1930 that the dust did not bother Filipino workers: "The white man can't stand the itch which results from working in the pear fields [the black soil] of the Delta. The dark skinned peoples are not affected by these conditions."[20] Waterman's opinion on the different skin color, which has been stereotypically used to differentiate racial minorities ideologically, reveals how the ideology of race has been instrumentalized in the U.S. capitalist system. The widespread ideology of race, which was produced within the political and economic context of U.S. capitalism, has been reproduced by media and has circulated like contagious rumor, and it also has provided U.S. employers with a justification for exploiting racial/ethnic minority workers.

However, when the employment opportunity gets scarce, the antagonism towards Filipinos becomes intense and mass media have spread the negative ideologies of Filipinos, calling them "savage," "criminal-minded," or "immoral," and blaming them for causing job competition. In *America*, Allos/Carlos depicts how negative stereotypes of racial/ethnic minorities have influenced people's perspectives on the different race and culture, and how the ideologies have reciprocally influenced the mind of racial/ethnic minorities themselves. Allos/Carlos writes,

> I put the blame on certain Filipinos who had behaved so badly in America, who had instigated hate and discontent among their friends and followers. This misconception was generated by a confused personal reaction to dynamic social forces, but my hunger for the truth had inevitably led me to take an historical attitude. I was to understand and interpret this chaos from a collective point of view, because it was pervasive and universal.[21]

Rejected, humiliated, and violently attacked by white Americans, Allos/ Carlos at first believes Filipinos' misconduct and pervasive racism to be the main reasons that Filipinos are discriminated against and treated badly in the United States. However, he gradually comes to understand the contradictory reality of U.S. capitalism, which recruits and exploits minority workers as cheap labor and then excludes them from society.

Thus Allos/Carlos comes to demystify what he has learned of "America" through the colonial education in the Philippines and decides to work for Filipino workers to educate them in how they have been conveniently exploited in the U.S. capitalist system: "They can't silence me any more! I'll tell the world what they have done to me!. . . . I *knew*-now. This violence had a broad social meaning."[22] It is also the moment that Allos/Carlos finds that Macario, who has demystified the illusion of "America" and become enlightened, starts calling him by his native name Allos again.

Allos's realization of the underlying economic mechanism and the contradictory U.S. capitalist system as well as discrimination along race/ ethnicity lines has brought him a social awakening and the courage to fight against injustice practiced against racial/ethnic minorities in the United States. Thus, Allos along with other Filipino laborers decides to demand equal wages and fair working conditions for minority workers. Filipino farm workers, who have endured unsanitary working and living conditions as well as daily punishments, realize that organizing themselves as a union is the only way to claim their rights. Allos helps to create an independent union, called the Filipino Workers' Association. Bulosan writes of the strong solidarity and growing class consciousness arising among Filipino workers as follows:

> The membership of the Filipino Workers' Association was tremendous,
> considering the myriad difficulties it met in the campaign to spread
> throughout the agricultural areas of California. The vigilant Filipino
> workers—their whole-hearted support of the trade union movement,
> their hatred of low wages and other labor discriminations—were the
> direct causes that instigated the persecutions against them, sporadic at
> first and then concerted, but destructive to the nation's welfare.[23]

The Filipinos' labor organization and their claim for equal wages was
regarded as a "violent" action, and U.S. capitalists' search for cheap labor
turned to different racial/ethnic groups, mainly to Mexican and other
laborers from Latin America. Later, social antagonism toward Filipinos
brought the passage of legislation in the Tydings-McDuffie Act of 1934.[24]
Recruited by U.S. demands for cheap labor, but excluded on account of
violent action and labor organization, Filipino workers became "exiles,"
who had left the Philippines, yet were not part of America.[25]

Allos's friend Joe comes to realize that racial discrimination against
minority workers in the United States is closely related to the political and
economic conflicts occurring in the process of U.S. capitalist development.
He explains to Allos how Filipino workers are caught in the conflict of
political economy of U.S. capitalism: "This is a war between labor and
capital. To our people, however, it is something else."[26] Joe's understanding of racist U.S. capitalism reveals that racially discriminating discourse
regarding minority workers has been used as an instrument to justify the
nation's economic demands for cheap labor as well as to stabilize the system by dividing laborers along race lines. Joe asserts the importance of
organizing a labor union, which is "broader," more "democratic," and
"all-inclusive," and of establishing class consciousness beyond racial/eth-
nic differences.

Allos comes to understand the larger underlying frame of the oppressive mechanism. His demystification of the illusion of "America" and his
realization of how the profit-oriented capitalist system has brought violent and inhumane treatment towards the colonized leads him to resist
what he has learned and idealized through the U.S. colonial education.
Allos's work for Filipinos' legal rights and his campaign for citizenship
reflect his realization of the predicament of Filipinos in the United States.
Filipino workers who were uprooted in their homeland, but economically
exploited and socially excluded in the United States, have felt in fact that
they have no place to go. Allos's social activities for education of Filipinos
and other minority workers and for expressing their rights in the United
States in which they have toiled reflect an effort to claim the alleged U.S.

"democratic" ideal, which is somewhere in the air but never fulfilled. Allos gives a speech to the Filipino workers:

> "We who came to the United States as immigrants are American too. All of us were immigrants—all the way down the line. We are American all who have toiled for this land, who have made it rich and free."
>
> Their eyes glowed with a new faith. They nodded with deep reverence. This was what I had been looking for in America! To make my own kind understand this vast land from our own experience.[27]

The noticeable point in Allos's speech is that he tries to read the history of "America" from the perspective of oppressed minorities who have worked for the country. Allos's notion of "America" as the land of immigrants who came here and worked hard to make the land better is an ideal version of "America." Although his experience in the United States is far different from the ideal image of "America," what Bulosan through Allos seeks is to close the gap between the racially discriminating American reality and the ideal version of "America."

Allos's work as a union organizer and editor of a union magazine as well as a representative of Filipino immigrants in the United States is his way of fighting against oppressive socioeconomic mechanisms and unequal power relations in society. Allos confronts the economic exploitation against racial/ethnic minorities in the U.S. capitalist system, and he demystifies the myth of "America" as an ideal place embodying democracy and equality. Through Allos's dissident voice, Bulosan highlights the conflict between capital and labor occurring in the developmental process of U.S. capitalism and reveals his critical awareness of how Filipino immigrants and other racial minority workers have been politically, economically, and ideologically exploited in U.S. labor markets.

Just as Bulosan ironically discloses the unfulfilled American reality through the title of the novel, *America* is Bulosan's interrogation of the contradictory U.S. capitalist system and discriminatory treatment towards minority immigrants. In the course of Allos's argument that the "advance of democracy was related to the working man's struggle for better wages and living conditions,"[28] Bulosan questions whether the "democratic" vision of "America" has been realized in reality. If U.S. multiculturalism's promotion of diversity is based on its "democratic" idea of racial/ethnic minorities, Bulosan's *America* reminds us of what needs to be further considered in order to fully appreciate the "democratic" meaning of "America" as a multiracial/cultural nation.

FROM "COOLIES" TO CHINATOWN SEAMSTRESSES: FAE MYENNE NG'S *BONE*

The claim for equal treatment and opportunities for racial/ethnic minorities that Bulosan has raised in *America Is In The Heart* also resounds in Ng's *Bone*. Unlike Jade Snow Wong's and Amy Tan's stories of Chinatowns, Ng's Chinatown is not displayed like "exhibited spectacles." Rather, Ng defamiliarizes the stereotypical view of Chinatowns and unravels the story as if peeling off the layers inside Chinatown, while putting the narrator Leila's half-sister Ona's suicide in the center of the plot.

> Looking out, I thought, So this is what Chinatown looks like from inside those dark Greyhound buses; this slow view, these strange color combinations, these narrow streets, this is what tourists come to see. I felt a small lightening up inside, because I knew, no matter what people saw, no matter how close they looked, our inside story is something entirely different.[29]

In *Bone*, there are no exotic spectacles exhibited for readers. Instead, Ng foregrounds a tragic incident that occurred in the 90s in San Francisco's Chinatown and develops her story while drawing attention to desperately struggling immigrants in ethnic communities. Leila, the narrator of the story, keeps asking, "why," to Ona's suicide and unravels the story as if investigating the cause of her death.

Unlike Tan's San Francisco Chinatown in *The Joy Luck Club,* which depicts relatively successful and well-settled Chinese immigrants, Ng's San Francisco Chinatown on Salmon Alley is replete with immigrants suffering from unstable economic conditions while being socially and economically confined in their ethnic enclaves. Connecting the historical exclusion of Chinese laborers to the bare lives of recent immigrants, Ng through *Bone* in a way leads us to rethink whether the legal abolition of Chinese Exclusion and the lifting of the bar against Asian immigrants after the mid-1960s have brought a significant difference to the lives of Asian immigrants. In other words, Ng through *Bone* reexamines the history of Chinese immigrants while connecting the immigrant past to the renewed social and economic exclusion that recent immigrants are experiencing.

The historical formation of Chinatown goes back to the 1880s, when anti-Chinese movements were intense and Chinese laborers were forced to move to other places and make their own ghettos to live in. The Chinese Exclusion Act of 1882 was enacted in the socioeconomic milieu of domestic laborers' fear of lowering wage due to employers' use of cheap immigrant laborers. Antagonism of the domestic working class toward racial/ethnic minorities increased to violence. Given this double layer of oppression, the options of Chinese laborers were severely limited. They were forced to turn inward to their own communities, and they found themselves segregated and excluded from white mainstream society.

In *Bone,* Ng interweaves the history of Chinese immigrants from the past to the present through the stories of Grandpa Leong, his paper son Leon, and Mah, who is working as a seamstress in Chinatown. Leon, the narrator Leila's stepfather, bears the experience of renewed social and economic exclusion against racial/ethnic minorities throughout his life. Leon was born in 1924, when the Chinese Exclusion Act was enacted, and he came to the United States in 1942, a year before the Chinese Exclusion Act was repealed. He came to the United States claiming to be the son of Leong, who somehow acquired U.S. citizenship. Leon had to buy a fake document in order to immigrate during the time that the Exclusion Act prevented the Chinese from entering the United States.

More than fifty years passed since Leon came to the United States as a paper son of Leong. Although legal discrimination against Asian immigrants was repealed a year after Leon arrived in the United States, what Leon has actually experienced as a cheap and temporary laborer proves that there is not much change in the socially excluded and economically exploited living conditions of Asian immigrants. Leon's experience as a temporary worker in harsh working conditions has made it hard for him to escape from the bottom of the economic scale. For Leon, "going back to China, only a bowl of bitterness to show for his life as a coolie," is a humiliation, and he realizes that his situation is not much different from Leong, who worked so hard but never returned to China with his dream of success.[30] In fact, the place where Leon finally ends up after the years of hard work and an unhappy marriage with Mah is the "same room he had when he was a bachelor going out to sea every forty days."[31] Ng, through the full circle of Leon's life, ironically reveals a continued suffering and exclusion that racial/ethnic minorities have experienced in U.S. capitalist society. Leon's failure to return Leong's "restless" bones to China in a way implies the deadlock circumstance in which Leon has been situated in the United States.

Leon feels "damned" for not keeping the promise with Leong. Thus he and Leila decide to find his bones, which are buried somewhere in a public cemetery. However, they find out that the bones are gone, and now it is "too late" to get them back. Ng, through the scene of searching for Leong's bones, leads us to trace back to the historical circumstance of Chinese "coolies." Just as Chinese immigrants were unrecognized and excluded from society, Leong's bones become "forgotten" and "abandoned." Ng indirectly connects Leon's failure to relocate Leong's bones to the broken bones of dead Ona: "The bones were lost, like Ona was lost."[32] Ona's suicide resulting from her being "stuck" and her dead body broken into pieces in a way resemble many Chinese laborers' unrepatriated bones, which are now all in boxes the "size of the Xerox boxes." Ona's suicide indicates her feeling of inescapability from her deadlocked situation. Connecting Leong's bones to Ona's, Ng draws attention to the historical and economic background of Chinese laborers as well as to the continuing economic suffering and social exclusion that recent immigrants are still experiencing in their confined ethnic communities.

Although Leon has lived in the United States since 1942, working as a seaman, houseboy, cook, busboy, or a servant for the whites, he has not achieved economic stability even after decades of hard work. His life has been socially and economically confined to Chinatowns. His suitcase is full of rejection letters saying, "We don't want you." Although the Chinese Exclusion Law was legally repealed in 1943, Leon's life is full of the bitterness of rejection and exclusion from society, and his bitter experience leads him to question whether any actually equal opportunity has been given to racial/cultural minorities in the United States after repeal of the Chinese Exclusion Act decades ago:

> Finally he blamed all of America for making big promises and breaking every one. Where was the good job he'd heard about as a young man? Where was the successful business? He'd kept his end of the bargain: he'd worked hard. Two jobs, three. Day and night. Overtime. Assistant laundry presser. Prep cook. Busboy. Waiter. Porter. But where was his happiness? "America," he ranted, "this lie of a country!"[33]

Leon discloses the gap between the racist reality and the myth of America as a "land of opportunity." His claim for justice and equality towards racial/ethnic minority workers resembles the desperate cry by Allos in *America Is In The Heart*. Just as Allos argued that Filipinos, who were recruited through U.S. employers' demands for cheap labor and were doubly exploited for their racially and nationally oppressed status in the United States, have their right to stay in the United States, so does Leon attempt to prove to the people that this country is his place too, because he had "earned his rights. American dollars. American time."[34]

Although the paper that Leon purchased at five thousand dollars from Leong allowed him to come to the United States, the legal identity of citizen in fact has not given Leon any social or economic security or stability. Leon has been frequently out of work in spite of his long hours of low-paying, hard work. Leon feels that he is not welcomed in the United States. When Leon applies for social security for retirement, he is being questioned for having many aliases and is denied for lack of documents to prove his "legal" eligibility. Leon, humiliated and angered, bursts out of the place and says, "I be in this country long time!"[35]

Upon Leon's failure to prove his identity, Leila decides to look through Leon's history. Looking into the suitcase where Leon has kept all papers and documents, Leila gradually understands Leon's paper history and his suffering from rejections saying "unfit," "unskilled," or "unavailable," which led him to believe that he does not belong to the society. The papers and documents that Leon has saved in a way tell the history of social and economic exclusion that racial minorities have experienced in the United States. The lie regarding his personal history was caused by the restrictive immigration law, enacted in 1924, which is ironically the year Leon was born according to the paper history. His feeling of insecurity and the continuous rejections and denial from society leaves him feeling bitter about "America." What Leon finally has left is "nothing but his anger."[36]

Understanding Leon's personal history in socioeconomic and legal contexts, Leila agrees with Leon's loathing towards ambivalent U.S. economic and legal policies and speaks to herself: "I never forget. I'm the stepdaughter of a paper son and I've inherited this whole suitcase of lies. All of it is mine. All I have are those memories, and I want to remember them all."[37] Leila comes to learn how Chinese laborers or racial minorities have been conveniently utilized and then denied to membership in society. Through Leila, Ng shows her critical awareness of the contradictory U.S. political and economic policies against racial/ethnic minorities and poses her dissident voice against oppressive legal and economic mechanisms with regard to minority immigrants.

The ambivalent treatment of immigrant workers in fact has continued throughout labor history. Ng, through Leon, expresses the way in which structural contradictions in the capitalist system are still shifting around racial/ethnic minorities. Ng thus emphasizes the effect of economic exploitation directed towards racial/ethnic minorities, an effect clearly still at work in U.S. labor markets. Leon was not able to mobilize himself economically, and his life is still confined to Chinatown. Failing to get a stable job on land, Leon would turn to unstable, dangerous jobs as a seaman and leave his family behind, just as in the old days Chinese men left China to work as "coolies" in the United States. Although Leon has lived more than five decades in the United States, he has yet to secure himself.

Unlike the popular ideology of Asian immigrants as a "model minority," who quickly settled down in the United States as middle class and moved away from ethnic communities, through Leon's unstable life in Chinatown, Ng challenges the myth of immigrant success. Foregrounding the tragic and painful stories occurred in the 1990s Chinatown, Ng draws attention to the underrepresented and poverty-stricken Chinese (or Asian) immigrants who are still struggling within the boundary of their ethnic communities, and she demystifies the media-propagated image of Asian immigrants as a "successful," "model" minority.

The case of Leila expresses an aspect of a continuous inequality forced on racial/ethnic minorities. Despite receiving a college education after she grew up in Chinatown, Leila was not successful in mobilizing herself outside her ethnic boundary. Working as a community relation specialist in Chinatown, she serves as a bridge between teachers and parents. Most of her students are recent immigrants, and she finds that the socially and economically marginalized ghetto condition in Chinatown is still continuing in the San Francisco Chinatown of the 90s.

> Being inside their cramped apartments depresses me. I'm reminded that we've lived like that, too. The sewing machine next to the television, the rice bowls stacked on the table, the rolled-up blankets, rearranged and used as stools or tables or homework desks. The money talk at dinnertime, the list of things they don't know or can't figure out. Cluttered rooms. Bare lives. Every day I'm reminded nothing's changed about making a life or raising kids. Everything is hard.[38]

Through her work, Leila comes to an awareness of the recent immigrants' living conditions in Chinatowns, where poverty and need-driven lives pervade. Talking with parents about the problems of recently immigrated students, Leila realizes that the immigrant parents are more in need of help than their children.

Chinatowns as ethnic enclaves signify the historical exclusion that has befallen the Chinese in the United States. Although several decades have passed since the Chinese Exclusion Act was repealed in 1943 and the legal restriction against Asians was abolished in 1965, bare life conditions in which many recent immigrants are situated reveal that they are still socially and economically marginalized in society.

The stereotypical images of Asian immigrants, who sacrifice their lives for the education of their children who become a "model" at school, are not found in Ng's *Bone*. Leila realizes that making a living, day by day, becomes much more important for them, and she sees that nothing much has changed in immigrants' lives in Chinatowns. Even when Leila and Nina—Leila's younger stepsister, who has moved from San Francisco to New York and works as a tourist guide—meet in New York and go out for dinner, Nina wants to avoid eating at Chinese restaurants, because everything related to Chinatown reminds her of a hard and bare life. Nina wishes she could at least enjoy a meal without feeling rushed. Leila agrees with Nina's feeling of bareness in Chinatown and decides to eat somewhere outside Chinatown. Their agreements in a way reflect their desperate wish to get out of the historically segregated and economically constricted ethnic enclaves. Through the depiction of poverty and need-driven life in Chinatowns, Ng reflects the continuing unequal power relations and structured inequality in society.[39]

Although formal legal discriminations against Asian immigrants were challenged after the mid-1960s, Leila finds that social and economic inequality is still at work, and economic disparity in society is increasing. To capture the widening economic gap among ethnic minorities, Ng in *Bone* portrays an aspect of class conflict among interethnic groups in depicting emotional tension between Mason, Leila's fiancé, and his cousin Dale, a computer whiz. Mason, who works as an auto mechanic, receives a request from his aunt Lily to fix her son Dale's BMW. Having fixed the car as a family favor, Mason delivers the car to Dale's home in the suburb of Redwood City. Dale grew up in a predominantly white community and speaks only English. Although Mason and Dale are cousins, Mason does not feel anything in common to share and communicate with him. "The guy [Dale] sounds so white," Mason says. Walking over to the glass doors, Mason and Leila see the "garden, the pool, the lollipop-colored lawn furniture."[40] What Mason and Leila see in Dale's house is apparently a class difference. Feeling uneasy listening to Dale's bragging about his successful company, Mason hurries to leave the house. Leila expresses her feeling of distance and class difference from Dale: "His house, his business, and even his smooth English all counted for something, but I knew I could never go with a guy like him. A guy with an uncallused smooth palm, a guy with Sunday hands."[41] Through this scene Ng depicts aspects of the increasing economic gaps and conflicts among interethnic groups. Dale has not grown up in Chinatown. His privileged status allowed him to go to an "all-white" school. Ng implies that Dale's relatively high-class position was not achieved by means of his excellent ability or his ethnic characteristics.

Asian immigrants' success is typically attributed to cultural characteristics such as diligence and hardworking attitudes. In *Bone,* however, Dale does not seem to have any of the "ethnic" qualities. Even though Mason fixes Dale's car as a family favor and drives the car to his house with his friends Zeke and Diana, who come along with another car to bring Mason back, Dale does not show much appreciation. Disappointed with Dale's poor manners, Leila comments:

> It sort of pissed me off to see Dale lounging by the pool after Mason'd spent all weekend under his car.
> "Dale should have thanked you too, Zeke," I said.
> Mason agreed. "For a computer wiz, the guy's sure stupid."
> "No manners," Zeke said. "Doesn't know how to treat people."
> "Family," I said.
> Diana said, "No home education."[42]

Ng cynically questions whether Dale, the successful computer whiz, has become a really successful "model" minority due to his excellent "ethnic" qualities.

Through the story of Dale, Ng challenges the media-propagated image of Asian immigrants as a myth, because the structured inequality in society has been inherited, and most immigrants have been economically constricted and their lives are still confined in ethnic enclaves. Although the ideology of Asian Americans as a "model minority" has been widespread since the 1960s, the media image of Asian immigrants as a "successfully" settled middle class in the United States has obfuscated the structural inequality in society. Moreover, the image of "successful" Asian Americans has underrepresented the reality of large numbers of minorities in impoverished conditions.

Class tension and conflicts among ethnic groups have actually increased, especially since various immigrant groups migrated to the United States after 1965. In *Bone*, Ona's suicide was partly the result of Leon's failure in his business partnership, Ong & Leong Laundry, which Leon started with Luciano Ong, who came from Peru. Leon cannot forgive Ong for cheating him and does not allow Ona to meet Ong's son, Osvaldo. When Luciano's wife, Rosa Ong, comes to Chinatown to work at the sweatshop where Mah works as a seamstress, most Chinese seamstresses do not trust her in view of her different ethnic background. However, Mah befriends her and teaches her how to sew. Later, their friendship develops and the idea of a business partnership develops between the two families.

In *Bone*, however, Ng does not simply treat Leon's failure in his business as a result of Ong's cheating on him and Ong's ethnically different quality. Instead, Ng draws a broader picture of the failure of Leon's business while connecting it to the ongoing change in composition in ethnic communities and increasing interracial conflicts and tensions: "Leong damned the day Luciano Ong came to Chinatown."[43] In other words, Ng portrays an aspect of ongoing changes in ethnic communities and increasing interethnic conflicts, which lead people to blame different ethnic characteristics rather than the overall economic structure that has placed minority workers in antagonistic relations.[44]

The question of why Ona killed herself is explored from the beginning of the story. Throughout the novel, Ng unravels the background stories of the incident as she investigates the cause. She does not, however, reduce Ona's death to a case of personal misjudgment. Although Ona's suicide is her own way of escaping from the deadlocked situation after her father Leon's failure in his business, Ng leads us to read the tragic incident in terms of broad social and economic circumstances that Leon's family has faced: "THE night everything finally blew up, I realized it had been inevitable."[45]

The inevitable conflicts among ethnic groups have recently increased in ethnic communities. Although systematic inequality in society and the exploitation of labor against racial/ethnic minorities are the main underlying reasons behind tension, prejudicial-sentiments have arisen targeting other ethnic minorities. Tensions and conflicts among racial/ethnic minorities become expressed as racism. Negative ideologies and widespread stereotypes of groups of people from different cultural and racial backgrounds have influenced people's way of thinking and their relationships with each other. Although Leon's failure in his business and the blame he assigns to Luciano as an untruthful partner depict one aspect of ethnic conflict occurring in ethnic communities, Ng in *Bone* tries to understand the conflict in a broad social and economic context. Ng implies that the cause of ethnic conflicts is related to the ongoing change in ethnic communities in which many racial/ethnic minorities work at low wages.

The ongoing restructuring of Chinatown or other ethnic communities reflects that the change is an extension of the capitalist logic of cheap labor. In the capitalist system, cheap labor can be assured through the hiring of racial and ethnic minorities, which will keep wages low. The pattern of the labor exploitation of racial minorities has continuously been functioning with dividing lines between race, ethnicity, and gender, and the ideological justification for stratifying the labor force according to racial and ethnic differences has served to maintain the class division and economic inequality in society. The main change in capitalists' exploitation of minority workers is that the demand for cheaper and more flexible labor was sought in a form of subcontracting by hiring mostly female workers in labor-intensive areas such as the garment industry.[46]

In *Bone*, Ng through Mah portrays how unhealthy working conditions and her strenuous sewing work under subcontracting have slowly destroyed her body and life style. Leila has watched her mother's changing body: "Her neck softened. Her shoulders grew heavy. Work was her whole life, and every forward stitch marked time passing."[47] Mah's physical change through her long years of sewing reflects an aspect of overexploitation of female laborers under subcontracting. Ng depicts the strenuous and time-driven working conditions of sweatshop factories under subcontracting as follows:

> Walking into the factory felt like walking into the cable-car barn. Every machine was running at high speed: the Singers zoomed, the button machines clicked. The shop vibrates like a big engine. Everything blended: oil and metal and the eye-stinging heat of the presses. The ladies pushed their endurance, long hours and then longer nights, as they strained to slip one more seam under the stamping needle.[48]

In *Bone*, Tommie Hom is the contractor of the sweatshop. Ng describes him as a "nervous wreck" yelling out the deadlines over the bells. Mah speeds up to sew another dozen to earn six dollars. Contractors, in a way, play a role as middlemen who exploit the labor of their own ethnic groups while supporting the larger economy of the society. Under subcontracting, employees are not legally protected and their wages depend on the pieces they complete. Based on individual contracts, subcontracting makes it easier for contractors to exploit laborers, who are mostly immigrant female workers working at cheap wages.[49]

Just as the recruitment of racial/ethnic minorities under the contracting system has brought an economic and ideological stability to the system, subcontracting as a renewed form of exploiting labor as well as a way to prevent labor organization has provided flexibility and more profit to U.S. capitalists. In *Bone*, Ng reveals how immigrant workers become contractors' convenient target for exploitation as cheap, "docile," and "flexible" labor, and she portrays the poor working conditions under subcontracting through Mah, who is already overburdened by her strenuous sewing work.

> Mah was too busy even to look up when I offered her her lunch. She said she didn't have an appetite, so I put the aluminum packet of food on the water pipe, where it'd stay warm, and her thermos on the already-filled communal eating table.
>
> She wanted to teach me to do zippers so I could sew another dozen for her at home. Mah's zippers were as flat and smooth as her seams. Speed was essential, but I could barely follow Mah's hands. She spun the dress pieces, and the needle was a blur, churning alongside the tracks of the zipper. The blue spool ripped over her head.

> Mah knew all the seams of a dress the way a doctor knows bones. She
> went quickly through the other parts: how to sew the darts, which she
> called "*the folds,*" when to sew all the connecting seams, called "*the big
> bones,*" and the special seams for the hems of each skirt, "*the feet.*"[50]

The important implication of the passage is that the literal meaning of
bones, which originally referred to the "coolie" Leong's "restless" bones,
is linked to Mah's sewing work. Through the metaphor of bones, Ng
reveals an aspect of the continuing exploitation of immigrant laborers from
"coolie" Chinamen of older times to the 90's San Francisco Chinatown
seamstress. The situation of contracted "coolies" as overexploited cheap
laborers is continued in the Chinese seamstress working at sweatshop factories under the subcontracting system. Just as Chinese "coolies" or Asian
immigrant laborers have been used to disintegrate labor unions and have
brought more profits to employers because of the exploitation of these
cheap laborers, the same principle of utilizing laborers along race/ethnicity
lines continues to be practiced towards recent immigrants, mostly female
laborers working as a labor-intensive workforce under the subcontracting
system.

In *Bone,* Ng portrays the disastrous and deadlock circumstances in
which most Asian immigrants are situated in the United States, in particular through Ona, whose body is totally exploded and broken. Just as Ona's
suicide resulted from an inescapable, deadlock feeling that she was "stuck
in the middle of the trouble,"[51] Ng, through Ona's exploded body, symbolically indicates an ongoing overexploitation of Asian immigrants.

In a departure from U.S. multiculturalism's focus on cultural characteristics of ethnic minorities, Ng's *Bone* represents a good example of an
Asian American multicultural text situated in the contexts of the historical
and ongoing restructuring of U.S. capitalism. The changing multiracial/eth-
nic composition in ethnic communities is a reflection of the continuing shifting of capital and labor around the availability of a cheap labor. Leon's and
Mah's personal experience and their struggle to survive in ethnic enclaves
are an example: the problem they had cannot simply be ascribed to their
personal and cultural situation. Rather, social and legal exclusions and the
structured inequality working against immigrant workers are the main reason that their lives have been put in such a difficult situation.

DIFFERENTIATED DIFFERENCE

In contrast with the majority of success stories and the politically acquiescent
voices that have dominated the well-received Asian American multicultural

literary scene, in this chapter I have drawn attention to politically conscious Asian American multicultural writings that focus on the "social structural component." As Bulosan's *America Is In the Heart* and Ng's *Bone* have depicted, the economic inequality and racial discrimination that minority workers have experienced in the United States is not caused by their biological and cultural differences. Rather, ethnic and racial differences have been utilized in domestic labor markets, and these differences as expressed in various negative stereotypes were utilized to justify hierarchized wages and labor divisions.

Stratification has been continued throughout U.S. history as shown in Bulosan's *America Is In The Heart* and Ng's *Bone*. In fact, the ongoing restructuring of U.S. capitalism has been continuously shifting around the availability of cheap labor, which reveals persistent inequality based on racial/ethnic differences. Keeping wages down or hiring a cheaper labor force becomes a means of creating surplus value in the capitalist system. In other words, inequality in labor markets helps to sustain the capitalist system and racial/ethnic minorities' differences are put to use in U.S. labor markets.

Bulosan's and Ng's multiracial/cultural texts addressed from the perspective of oppression are examples of Asian American multicultural writings breaking out of the narrow spectrum of popular and mystified multiculturalism. These literary works represent an oppositional voice against the politically assimilated and acquiescent Asian American multicultural literature. Both Bulosan and Ng delineate a critical awareness of Asian immigrants' social and economic status and position as "unassimilable aliens," "savages," "coolies," or as a "model minority," which were ideologically woven through the complex interactions of capital and labor in U.S. labor markets. Bulosan's and Ng's foregrounding of socially and economically marginalized groups and the depiction of the struggles of oppressed immigrants, "coolies," or Chinatown seamstresses indirectly challenge the dominant ideology and stereotypical image of Asian immigrants as a "docile" and "successful" minority. What Bulosan's and Ng's politically conscious multicultural texts delineate is a counternarrative to the structured inequality and unequal power relations working against racial/ethnic minorities in society. The critical voice embedded in Bulosan's *America Is In The Heart* and Ng's *Bone* is an interrogation of the U.S. capitalist system and the authors' way of fighting back against the oppressive structure of U.S. society.

Chapter Four

Is There Any Essential Component of Asian American Literature?: Karen Tei Yamashita's *Tropic of Orange*

This sociality of multiculturalism is historically specific to late capitalism. So it is necessary in the process of ethnical and political judgment
to grasp the ways in which the concept of value and its forms is theo-
rized in the political economy of commodity production as an episte-
mological framework in assaying the worth of culture.

—E. San Juan Jr., *Beyond Postcolonial Theory*

Karen Tei Yamashita's first novel *Through the Arc of the Rain Forest*
(1990) received the Before Columbus Foundation American Book Award
and the Janet Heidinger Kafka Prize, yet the work has not been "popularly" acknowledged by the reading public or in academic circles. Claudia
Sadowski-Smith in her article on transnationalism in fiction suggests that it
may be because Yamashita does not situate her novel within her "own ethnic
community" and because her text is "explicitly anti-capitalist."[1] King-Kok
Cheung has asserted that Yamashita's *Through the Arc of the Rain Forest*
does not belong to the category of Asian American literature, because the
novel is not situated in North America and does not "dwell on being Asian
or Asian American."[2] These criticisms raise interesting questions: "Should"
Asian American writers reflect ethnicity-specific issues through their writings? Is there any essential component of Asian American literature?

Although Asian American identity does not conform to a rigid notion
of binary identity formation, the expectation of many readers and critics
regarding "ethnic" elements in Asian American writings implies a renewed
inflexibility regarding Asian Americans and Asian American literature.
Hence Yamashita charges that "the notion of what is Asian-American must

89

change," and she attempts to demystify the stereotype of Asian Americans as "essentially" different "ethnic others."[3]

Despite the 1960s' critical racial movement and the fact that in many cases the migration of Asian immigrants to the United States after 1965 has been a consequence of the political and economic instability of their countries of origin and the ideological influence of U.S. domination,[4] many popularly received literary works produced by Asian immigrant/Asian American writers after 1965 are politically disengaging and mostly silent about the political and economic conditions that have brought the people to the United States. Rather, the popularly acknowledged Asian immigrant/ Asian American writers have shown some commonalities in dealing with politically neutral and culturally distinctive subjects. Notwithstanding Lisa Lowe's depiction of the phenomenon of Asian migration to the U.S. as the "return to the imperial center" and her reading of Asian immigrants as "critical subjects," who refuse to identify themselves as "faithful" U.S. citizens,[5] it has been the case that most widely-received Asian American writings are filled with politically "interpellated," "good" subjects, which are faithful to the U.S. ideological identification of Asian Americans as a "docile," "model minority." In other words, there are some gaps between the literary representations produced by Asian immigrant/Asian American writers and the "collective memories of imperialism" that many Asians/Asian immigrants bear. It cannot be generalized, however, that most Asians, as Lowe argues, share a perspective on the U.S. domination of their countries—for U.S. infiltration of other countries was often made possible through an alliance with the dominant group of the country, and the Immigration Act of 1965, which has given a visa preference to professionals in science and technology and to investors, has filtered mostly the upper middle class into the United States, thus layering a socioeconomic hierarchy among immigrants in terms of class. The gap between literary representation and actual memory essentially has been sealed or masked by the stories that tout Asian immigrants' success and distinctive Asian cultural characteristics. These are the aspects foregrounded in most politically acquiescent Asian American writings. Moreover, the stereotypical view of Asian Americans as "cultural others" or a "docile," "model" minority has been unchallenged, and the image of Asian Americans has been continuously renewed within the existing ideological identification of Asian Americans.

Yamashita's *Tropic of Orange*, which was published in 1997, is her effort to challenge highly stereotypical ideological assumptions regarding Asian American literature. It is her critique of an essentialized view of racial/ethnic minorities. *Tropic of Orange* is based in Los Angeles—a multicultural/racial metropolis that embodies a specific material site of conflicts around racial/ethnic immigrants—and it foregrounds racial/ethnic minorities in the core of the novel. Yamashita indeed has crafted the story around seven characters, each belonging to racial/ethnic "minorities" in the United States. By weaving her story with diverse characters from different racial, cultural, and economic backgrounds, Yamashita challenges the white middle-class dominant perspective of "American" society and unravels her vision of U.S. multicultural society while investigating political, ideological, and economic conflicts involving racial/ethnic immigrants. Her text fully engages political and economic contexts in order to call attention to the underlying grid of the multiracial/cultural map of "America."

"MULTICULTURALISM IS EVERYWHERE, YET MULTICULTURALISM IS NOWHERE"

In *Tropic of Orange,* Yamashita's challenge of the rigid notion of identity and ethnicity is portrayed through a character, Bobby Ngu, who is "Chinese from Singapore with a Vietnamese name speaking like a Mexican living in Koreatown."[6] Bobby's identity cannot be properly defined within a binary-opposed traditional category of identification: it exemplifies a multidefined identity. Living in Koreatown, Bobby watches Korean television programs and enjoys listening to their different sounds. Bobby is a figure representing a changing characteristic in ethnic communities, just as Ng's Chinatown has shown a changing ethnic composition mixed with Chicanos and other Latin Americans.

Depicting Bobby's backgrounds and his reason for migrating to the United States, Yamashita implicitly links the phenomenon of Asian migration to U.S. capitalist expansionism towards Asian countries. Bobby used to be in the middle class in Singapore, but had to leave the country due to his father's failure in his business. Following his father's advice, at age twelve Bobby comes to the U.S. by disguising himself as a Vietnamese war refugee. Bobby explains the reason he had to immigrate:

> Dad had a factory. Putting out bicycles. Had a good life. Good money. Only had to go to school. One day, American bicycle company put up a factory. Workers all went over there. New machines. Paid fifty cents more. Pretty soon, American company's selling all over. Exporting. Bicycles go to Hong Kong. Go to Thailand. To India. To Japan. To Taiwan. Bobby's dad losing business. Can't compete. That's it.[7]

Bobby's reason for immigration reflects how U.S. economic penetration to other worlds has disrupted the indigenous economy and the people's means of living. In consequence, the drifting of the uprooted people and labor migration have become a common phenomenon in capitalist society. Bobby's immigration to the United States indirectly stands for the "return" of the uprooted to the center of the empire. Bobby starts his new life in the United States from the bottom of the economic rung, sorting out tons of mail in the daytime and managing his own cleaning business at night. Although Bobby is part of the underrepresented Asian immigration and his migration to the U.S. is related to U.S. capitalist expansionism towards Asian countries, he does not read the phenomenon of migration as a part of capitalist development, and he does not consciously respond to how minority immigrants are being utilized as cheap labor in domestic labor markets. Instead, he disagrees with his wife Rafaela's joining in a demonstration against unfair treatment of janitors. Bobby's attitude and perspective in a sense reveal a stereotypical image of Asian immigrants who are "diligent" and "work hard" to achieve economic success, but remain politically disengaged and conservative.

Rafaela, conversely, who is Mexican American and has her college degree from an L.A. community college, is politically conscious about belonging to a minority in the United States. She knows the importance of organizing power against the exploitative system and critically reacts to unequal power relations and the structural inequality practiced against racial/ethnic minorities in U.S. society. Rafaela urges Bobby to be more consciously aware of how minorities are differentiated in U.S. labor markets and to respond to the systematic exploitation through organized action:

> She [Rafaela] told Bobby, janitors like them got to make better money. Got to get benefits. Some don't even get the minimum. Can we live on $4.25 an hour? No way. She joined Justice for Janitors. Bobby got mad. This is his business. He's independent. All the money is his. What's she talking about? It's solidarity she said. Some work for the companies. They need to organize. For protection. Bobby don't understand this. He says he works the morning job and gets benefits. Why is she complaining?[8]

Whereas Rafaela critically reacts to ideological misrepresentation and economic exploitation of racial/ethnic immigrants, Bobby prefers to conform to the existing system. While Rafaela interprets working without protection as an economic exploitation and argues that it is necessary to ask for fair treatment, Bobby reacts as if he naturally accepts the existing unequal power relation along race/ethnicity lines in U.S. labor markets. Contrasting the different political stances of Bobby and Rafaela, Yamashita indirectly criticizes the politically conservative Asian immigrants, who are regarded as a "non-threatening" group, yet are still a "disempowered" minority in the United States.

Yamashita's efforts to raise a critical awareness and her criticism of "docile" and system-conforming Asian Americans are highlighted through Emi, a Japanese American journalist. Proclaiming herself as "distant from the Asian female stereotype,"[9] Emi directly resists the dominant stereotype engraved on Asian Americans. She criticizes the typical image of Asian Americans as technical workers, who live within the "touted" image of Asian immigrants as "model" minority. Emi cynically says, "If you are making a product you can actually touch *and*, . . . making a comfortable living at it, you are either an Asian or a machine."[10] Through this passage Yamashita makes fun of a predominant image of Asian immigrants, who are politically conforming like a "machine," yet have "survived" economically.

Yamashita indicates the necessity of forming an interethnic collaboration beyond rigid racial/ethnic boundaries and emphasizes that it is important for Asian Americans to react critically to the stereotypical image imposed on them. Emi's conscious attempt to move beyond the stiff boundary of race and ethnicity is revealed through her personal relationships. Emi's boyfriend Gabriel, a news reporter, is a Chicano who was very much influenced by the 1960s' Chicano movement and who tries to follow the good example of critical intellectuals. Emi is cynical about the way in which multiculturalism in the United States has been acknowledged, that is, as a merely "cognitive" understanding of differences. She speaks directly about her opinions of multiculturalism to Gabriel at a sushi bar:

"Do you know what cultural diversity really is?" [Emi asks]

"I am thinking." [Gabriel replies]

"It's a white guy wearing a Nirvana T-shirt and dreds. That's cultural diversity." Emi looked up at the sushi chef. "Don't you hate being multicultural?" she asked.

"Excuse me?"

The woman next to Emi bristled under her silk blouse and handcrafted silver. She looked apologetically at the sushimaker and said, "Hiro-san, having a hard day?"

"Hiro," Emi butted back in. "I hate being multicultural."

"Can't you calm down?" The woman never looked at Emi, but offered up a patronizing smile for Hiro-san. "We are trying to enjoy our tea. By the way, Hiro-san, it's just delicious today."

"See what I mean, Hiro? You're invisible. I'm invisible. We're all invisible. It's just tea, ginger, raw fish, and a credit card."[11]

Emi's strong aversion to cultural diversity in a sense reveals the way in which multiculturalism in the United States has been acknowledged, that is as a merely cognitive understanding of differences. From Emi's perspective, ongoing discussion of U.S. multiculturalism is not much different from consuming and appreciating culturally different ethnic products and commodities, which could be construed as another euphemism for a market ideology supporting capitalist expansionism beyond the current boundaries.

Emi's strong disagreement with U.S. multiculturalism's promotion of cultural diversity is related to its institutionalized and commercialized trends. Emi's opinion of cultural diversity as an ideological discourse of capitalism is clearly expressed in her conversation with Gabriel:

> It's just about money. It's not about good honest people like you or about whether us Chicanos or Asians get a bum rap or whether third world countries deserve dictators or whether we should make the world safe for democracy. It's about selling things: Reebok, Pepsi, Chevrolet, AllState, Pampers, Pollo Loco, Levis, Fritos, Larry Parker Esq., Tide, Raid, the Pillsbury Doughboy, and Famous Amos.[12]

What Yamashita through Emi argues is that U.S. multiculturalism's promotion of cultural diversity plays the role of cultural brokering for U.S. multinational/transnational trade under the slogan, "We are the world."

Indeed, the way multiculturalism is promoted in the United States is not much different from the market ideology of fostering consumerism. For instance, when Bobby brings his alleged Chinese cousin from Mexico to the United States, the cousin has to cross the U.S.-Mexican border, which has become another route for Asians to enter the United States. Bobby realizes that his cousin needs to be dressed up with "American" styles in order to pass the border, and he gradually understands what being a racial/ethnic minority means in the United States. When Bobby smuggles his Chinese cousin into the United States, he realizes that everything that looks as if it is racially and ethnically different becomes associated with the notion of illegality. Thus he tries to get rid of his cousin's ethnic difference by consuming U.S. multinational commodities:

> Bobby takes the little cuz to a T.J. beauty shop. Get rid of the pigtails. Get rid of the Chinagirl look. Get a cut looking like Rafaela. That's it. Now get her a T-shirt and some jeans and some tennis shoes. Jean say Levi's. Shoes say Nike. T-shirt says Malibu. That's it. . . . He's got the cuz holding a new Barbie doll in a box, like she bought it cheap in T.J. Official eyeballs Bobby's passport and waves them through. That's it.

Two celestials without a plan. Drag themselves through the slit jus' like
any Americanos. Just like Visa cards.[13]

By consuming U.S. commodity brands, by dressing up like other "Americans," and by erasing ethnic differences by means of a homogenized "American" look, Bobby's Chinese cousin successfully crosses the border as if they
were a father and daughter coming back to the States from Mexico. Being
identified as "American" in U.S. capitalist society in a sense equates with
the ability to purchase multinational commodities, or with having a homogenized look based on U.S. "multinational brands." Bobby's cousin, who has
consumed U.S. multinational brand names, thus "legally" passes the border without being scrutinized, and her consumed "American" look comes
to be substituted as her identity and legal status. Yamashita in the passage
interestingly connects legal "visa" to a "Visa card," which "demonstrates
the particular border-crossing fluidity of capital."[14] The "collapse of the difference between visas and Visa cards," as Molly Wallace points out, in fact
signifies an aspect of "postnational" global capitalism: " 'American,' here,
comes to mean American consumerism; 'nationality' is a brand-name."[15]

Through the border-crossing scene, Yamashita implicitly questions
whether promoting cultural diversity signifies appreciating differences in
race and culture, or whether it is merely a convenient password for trans-
nationalizing capital serving as an ideological mouthpiece for globalizing U.S. capitalism. Although cultural diversity has been promoted in the
name of multiculturalism, the slogan is just floating around without fulfill-
ing its democratic substance. What U.S. multiculturalism has promoted
thereby becomes suspect, and Yamashita interrogates the ideology behind
this multiculturalism.

DISPOSSESSED RACIAL/ETHNIC
MINORITIES AS THE HOMELESS

Despite its apparent diverse racial/ethnic composition, California, where
many racial/ethnic immigrants have worked as cheap labor, has continuously been a conflicted site: racial tension and exclusion movements were
more harsh and severe towards racial/ethnic immigrants here than any-
where else in the United States. One of the disastrous incidents occurring
in California was the Japanese internment during World War II. As this
case reveals, California has a dark underbelly beneath its colorful rainbow
surface. Yamashita portrays the ambivalent rhetoric and exclusionary treatment of minority immigrants in California through a character called Manzanar, a homeless Sansei (the third generation of Japanese immigrants).

Manzanar used to be a surgeon, but he gave up his job and became a voluntary homeless person conducting imaginary music on highways. He creates his name Manzanar out of his birthplace, "Manzanar Concentration Camp in the Owens Valley," where he was born during World War II.[16] As the name Manzanar implies, Yamashita symbolically connects the image of interned Japanese to disenfranchised racial/ethnic immigrants, unveiling the violent treatment of Japanese immigrants during the war. What Manzanar keeps in his little camp—some books, magazines, a lantern, cooking utensils, bedding, a change of clothing, and soap—in a way reminds us of what Japanese immigrants had in internment camps.

Yamashita also investigates the background to Japanese internment in West coast areas during World War II and emphasizes an economic aspect behind the political reason for internment.[17] As a character in Okada's *No-No Boy* (1957) has argued, the real reason that the Japanese living on the West Coast (not the Japanese in Hawaii) have become a target for internment is economic competition between the Japanese and Californians, especially in the agricultural business.[18]

Yamashita uses the homeless Manzanar to question implicitly and explicitly the ideological justification for the Japanese having been interned and the violent confiscation of their properties in the name of national security. In Yamashita's view, the violent treatment of Japanese immigrants in the name of protecting U.S. citizens is not much different from the way society treats the homeless as economically undesirable and "expendable" in society. Like the violent removal of the homeless, who have no right to claim property without paying for it under the capitalist system, Japanese immigrants, regarded as a "dangerous" and "undesirable" element, were violently excluded from "American" society. Manzanar's forming a homeless encampment called Los Angeles Poverty Department (L.A.P.D.) in this respect is his particular protest against the unfair treatment of Japanese immigrants, which has left them just like the economically dispossessed. His decision to be homeless even after the internment years is a product of his strong disagreement with U.S. exclusionary attitudes towards racial/ethnic minorities, which is still going on underneath the colorful multiracial/cultural surface.

As Yamashita says, "the homeless weren't going away."[19] Despite being regarded as "undesirable" in society, the homeless have continuously existed as if the capitalist system itself needs them for sustaining the structure. In a similar manner, labor migration from Asia and Latin America to the United States has continued despite the media's spreading of anti-immigrant sentiments towards racial/ethnic immigrants. In other words, Yamashita reveals a double or rather contradictory rhetoric that the United

States has posed against racial/ethnic minorities—exploiting them economically, while using them ideologically.

In addition, Yamashita challenges the conservative and conforming attitudes that many Japanese immigrants themselves have displayed after the internment years. Manzanar's previous job as surgeon shows that he is an example of a "model" Asian American. However, Manzanar's giving up his job implies his reaction against the dominant "model minority" image:

> To say that Manzanar Murakami was homeless was as absurd as the work he chose to do. No one was more at home in L.A. than this man. The Japanese American community had apologized profusely for this blight on their image as the Model Minority. They had attempted time after time to remove him from his overpass, from his eccentric activities, to no avail.[20]

Despite Manzanar being Emi's grandfather, Emi has not known about him because her family has felt ashamed of his being homeless and did not want to talk about him. Portraying Emi's family and the Japanese American community's politically silent attitudes, Yamashita criticizes most Asian Americans' subservient and ideologically conforming gesture to U.S. society. Manzanar's being homeless is thus his refusal to be identified with other ideologically conservative Japanese Americans as well as his critique of internal conflicts among Japanese communities after the war.

By being a "grassroots conductor," demystifying the ideology tagging Asian Americans as a "model minority," Manzanar becomes an example of a critically reacting and politically conscious Asian American. The music that Manzanar conducts on freeways in a way leads us back to when immigrant workers built the economic foundation of the present freeway system. Yamashita reminds us of how the city has been built upon backbreaking labor by minority immigrants:

> There was a time when the V-6 and the double-overhead cam did not reign. In those days, there were the railroads and the harbors and the aqueduct. These were the first infrastructures built by migrant and immigrant labor that created the initial grid on which everything else began to fill in. . . . Spread across these infrastructures was yet another of Manzanar's grids: his map of labor. It was those delicate vulnerable creatures within those machines that made this happen: a thing called work. Every day, he saw them scatter across the city this way and that, divvying themselves up into the garment district, the entertainment industry, the tourist business, the military machine, the service sector,

the automotive industry, the education industry, federal, county, and city employees, union workers, domestics, and day labor. It was work that defined each person in the city, despite the fact that almost everyone wanted to be defined by their leisure.[21]

Yamashita in this passage clearly puts forward how people are conditioned by their labor in the capitalist system and how racial/ethnic minorities have been utilized as cheap labor in the United States without being appreciated. Manzanar's mapping of immigrants' backbreaking labor foregrounds the historical and economic foundation of U.S. capitalist society through exploitation of minority immigrants.

Through Manzanar's "laboring choir," Yamashita disseminates the underrepresented and marginalized voices of minority immigrants. Manzanar's mapping of labor in this regard is his way of calling attention to the disenfranchised minority as well as of questioning U.S. multiculturalism, which celebrates cultural diversity while covering up the fundamental and structural inequality practiced against racial and ethnic minorities.

"THE WORLD DRINKS COKE"—MULTICULTURAL/ NATIONAL DISCOURSE OF GLOBALIZATION

While the incident of Japanese internment during World War II stands as an example of U.S. contradictory treatment of immigrants, Yamashita suggests that a cyclical pattern of recruitment and exclusion of minority immigrants is ongoing. Although minority immigrants have suffered discrimination for their race and ethnicity in U.S. labor markets and although they have been utilized for the system's sake by being paid at a less than minimum wage, the widespread stereotype of minority immigrants in general has always been associated with the negative image of "illegal."[22] Yamashita speaks against the widely distributed negative images of minority immigrants and undocumented immigrants as "intolerable burdens," "racial and cultural contaminants," "free-loaders," and "welfare cheats."[23] Although the presence of immigrants in the United States has always been blamed as a cause of social and economic problems, U.S. economic demand for cheap labor has never ceased and racial/ethnic minorities have been recruited through various means.[24]

Yamashita portrays a renewed example of the U.S. ambivalent rhetoric of immigrants through an incident of "orange scare." Oranges, which were "recommended for boosting mental and muscular activity," are suddenly banned as "illegal" for injected chemicals: "Everybody down south being looked into. Oranges went underground. The word was emphatic:

All oranges were suspect. And deemed highly toxic. . . . See an orange? Call 911."[25] Yamashita in a humorous way connects the incident of orange scare to the negative image tagged on minority immigrants—especially Mexicans and other Latin Americans in recent years—as "illegal" or "undesirable trespassers" in the United States.

Through the scene of the illegal orange incident, Yamashita parodies the current phenomenon of Mexicans' movement north and the media distribution of negative images on minority immigrants in general. The widespread image of Mexicans as "illegal" aliens has indeed built a racial and ethnic antagonism in the current economic crisis, and their presence in the United States has been regarded as the source of "high unemployment" and "rising cost of social welfare." Despite racial/ethnic minorities being economically exploited as cheap labor, their presence in U.S. society has been politically and ideologically utilized as a putative cause of social and economic problems. In fact, their negative label as "illegal" has put them to work underground or at home as a flexible labor force, which means that their labor is unorganized and they have to work without benefits or protection.[26] In other words, restrictive legal policies and the media distribution of negative images of racial/ethnic immigrants, especially Latinos in recent years, have contributed to a further exploiting of racial/ethnic minority's labor, while scapegoating them as the source of current economic crises.

Historically, the state of California was once a part of Mexico. After the U.S. colonization of the northern part of Mexico, Mexicans' migration north became inevitable, yet the redrawing of the border has transformed the indigenous people's migration north into an "illegal" border crossing. The northward movement of Mexicans has resulted from U.S. colonization of northern Mexico as well as U.S. political and economic domination of Mexico. As Gloria Anzaldua has pointed out, Mexicans' migration north has been a historical movement like a "tradition," which has come out of "economic desperation." Thus Anzaldua calls "mojados" (wetbacks) "economic refugees."[27]

In *Tropic of Orange*, Yamashita supplies a vivid image of the uprooted Latin Americans through a character called Arcangel. This character is portrayed as a prototypical figure embodying a historical consciousness of Latin America.[28] He has come "from a long away, from the very tip of the Tierre del Fuego, from Isla Negra. . . . And yet his voice was often a jumble of unknown dialects guttural and whining, Latin mixed with every aboriginal, colonial, slave, or immigrant tongue, a great confusion discernible to all and to none at all."[29] As a living historical figure of the past and the present of Latin America, Arcangel moves to the north as if it is his "manifest destiny."

Yamashita portrays a scene where Archangel on his journey north stops at a local bar in Mexico, named "Misery & Hunger" and is surprised at people drinking only American beers. Arcangel does not understand how this has happened and asks the waiter in the bar:

> "All American beers. But we are in Mexico, are we not? Where are the Mexican beers?"
>
> "Perhaps you would prefer Coca-Cola or Pepsi?"
>
> "Perhaps I would like a hamburger, Fritos, and catsup."
>
> "It is our special today."
>
> It was true. Arcangel looked around at all the hungry and miserable people in the cantina—all eating hamburgers, Fritos, catsup, and drinking American beers. Only he, who had asked the cook the favor of cooking his raw cactus leaves, ate nopales.[30]

Yamashita has visualized how deeply Mexico and other countries in South America have been impacted by U.S. economic domination and have become the commodity markets for the United States. The border between North and South has been continuously shifting, and the changing geography reflects a continuously expanding movement of U.S. capitalism.

As a way of showing resistance to the homogenizing U.S. capitalist system throughout the world, Yamashita sketches a figure, El Gran Mojado, as a transformation of Arcangel, and has him confronted with SUPERNAFTA, a personification of U.S. capitalist expansionism. Arcangel/El Gran Mojado is a figure embodying Latin history and Latino spirit. In a defiant voice Arcangel/El Gran Mojado recites a conflicting history of Latin America:

> *Have you forgotten 1848 and the*
> *Treaty of Guadalupe Hidalgo?*
> *With a stroke of the pen,*
> *Mexico gave California to the gringos.*
> *The following year,*
> *1849,*
> *everyone rushed to get the gold in California,*
> *and all of you Californians who were already there*
> *and all of you indigenas who crossed*
> *and still cross the new border*
> *for a piece of the gold have become*
> *wetbacks.*
> *My struggle is for all of you.*

El Gran Mojado derives his great strength
from the noble hearts of his people!
Let's see if this SUPERSCUMNAFTA is not a
coward!
He is only concerned with the
commerce of money and things.
What is this compared to the great
commerce of humankind? [31]

Yamashita interrogates how U.S. territorialization of northern Mexico has changed the status of most Mexicans into "illegal" border trespassers, and how unfair economic agreements between the two countries have eventually uprooted most Mexicans and have caused Mexicans' unavoidable migration to the center of the empire.

Thus, Yamashita derides NAFTA's "free trade,"[32]which sounds "liberating," but eventually has brought more debts to the people in the country and has deepened Mexico's economic dependence on the United States.

IMF debts.
Loans and defaults.
A twenty-eight billion dollar trade deficit?
Devaluate the peso.
A miracle?
No more debt for the country. Instead
personal debt for all its people.
Free trade.[33]

Arcangel/El Gran Mojado recites in a cynical manner how unequal commercial trade through NAFTA has gradually destroyed the economic means of Mexicans and eventually left them uprooted from their homeland.[34] Without paying tariffs under the free economic trade agreement of NAFTA, U.S. products could go beyond national boundaries much more easily, which has eventually helped the United States to expand its commodity markets to other worlds.

The predatory nature of U.S-centered capitalist expansionism under NAFTA's free trade policy is concealed in the term "free," which sounds positive while hiding the greedy and violent nature behind it. Yamashita clearly expresses how the progressive capitalist logic has violently subsumed pre-capitalist or "less-developed" countries under the U.S. capitalist system and disrupted the indigenous culture and economy. Critically engaging the ambivalent aspect of capitalism, Yamashita demystifies the myth of capitalism as a "liberating" and "free" economic system. Arcangel/El Gran Mojado cynically states the underlying ideology of the capitalist system:

> *The myth of the first world is that*
> *development is wealth and technology progress.*
> *It is all rubbish.*
> *It means that your are no longer human beings*
> *but only labor.*
> It means that the land you live on is not earth
> *but only property.*
> *It means that what you produce with your own hands*
> *is not yours to eat or wear or shelter you*
> *if you cannot buy it.*[35]

In the passage, Yamashita seeks to question whether the capitalist system has brought more freedom to people or has instead made people more enslaved by capital. In other words, Yamashita interrogates the manner in which the capitalist system has spread its expansionist logic while justifying itself with the myth of progress and liberation, and how the progressive capitalist logic has destroyed indigenous culture and the native economic system.

Yamashita's depiction of violent U.S. capitalist expansionism toward other worlds is personalized through the character SUPERNAFTA, a "cold and cruel looking white guy from North America." Painting an image of SUPERNAFTA as cruel and greedy, Yamashita parodies the violent penetration and domination of other worlds through the unfair economic agreement of NAFTA. As a way of resisting U.S. capitalist expansionism, Yamashita depicts a wrestling match between Arcangel/El Gran Mojado and SUPERNAFTA.

The Pacific Rim Auditorium at Borders, the place in which the wrestling match is taking place, also has a metaphorical meaning that signifies U.S. capitalist expansionism around the Pacific Rim. Like the spread of the U.S.-centered capitalist system all over the world, SUPERNAFTA's posters are everywhere in the Auditorium. The fight between Arcangel/El Gran Mojado and SUPERNAFTA in a sense symbolizes a long historical tension between the Americas. The wrestling match is regarded as an epochal event and is expected to be a violent and bloody fight. In the wrestling match, Arcangel/El Gran Mojado manages to stand his ground and succeeds in having SUPERNAFTA implode. However, the final weapon that SUPERNAFTA has in his finger—a missile launcher—penetrates Arcangel/El Gran Mojado's heart before SUPERNAFTA collapses. The fight between them has been a breathtaking moment for the audiences in the Pacific Rim Auditorium, and it ends disastrously for both contenders. The wrestling match is symbolic in that it denotes a grassroots movement against U.S. political and economic domination of Mexico and other worlds. By posing SUPERNAFTA as an opponent of Arcangel/El Gran Mojado, Yamashita shows that resistance to U.S. imperialist domination of the world is arising.

MULTICULTURALISM RECONSIDERED: "CULTURAL DIVERSITY IS BULLSHIT"

What distinguishes Yamashita's *Tropic of Orange* from other Asian American multicultural literary works, such as Wong's *Fifth Chinese Daughter* and Tan's *The Joy Luck Club*, is the author's conscious reaction to the systematic discrimination and power inequality along race/ethnicity lines as well as her broad perspective reading the issues of migration of labor and capital within global capitalist contexts. Yamashita in an interview with Murashige indicates: "I can say only that I want to write about it with some honesty and integrity. I would find it hard to write a book without ideas, without political content, or without a vision. I would find it hard to simply write about some family saga. I guess the answer is more in creating the questions, creating an awareness."[36] As Yamashita has clearly expressed, she is a conscious writer paying attention to the marginalized and underrepresented minorities, and her critical investigation of the political, ideological, and economic conflicts surrounding minority immigrants calls attention to the issues that lie beyond ethnicity. What Yamashita attempts through her writings is to raise a critical racial consciousness beyond ethnicity.

At this point I would like to recur to the criticisms directed at Yamashita by Sadowski-Smith and Cheung as noted in the beginning of this chapter. I would argue that their objections to Yamashita's not situating her novel within her "own ethnic community" and not "dwelling on being Asian or Asian American" reveal some limitation in their understanding of Asian American literature. It seems to me that their reading of Asian American literature as "ethnicity-specific" is inflexible and their perspectives on Asian American literature have not risen above the boundary of ethnicity. Being Asian Americans does not mean that authors have to dwell on their status as a racial/ethnic minority. On the contrary, articulating racial/ethnic difference should be an attempt to frame the issue of discriminatory policies against minorities in society, and what Asian Americans or Asian American writers should do is move beyond the boundaries of ethnic differences and develop a sense of critical consciousness. In fact, what Yamashita consciously challenges is the very ideologies commonly associated with Asian American literature as the representation of "essentially different ethnic others."

Yamashita's emphasis on the necessity of forming a political alliance beyond ethnic differences is well conveyed through her portrayal of the L.A. uprising of 1992. Yamashita says in an interview that she started writing *Tropic of Orange* in 1991, and that a year later she observed an increasing conflict among ethnic groups, especially between African Americans and Korean immigrants.[37] Mass media has labeled it the "L.A. riots" and has placed the blame on each ethnic group rather than on the unequal social and economic structure of society. In *Tropic of Orange,* Yamashita depicts the historical incident and its disastrous impact on ethnic communities through Celia Oh, a Korean Brazilian, who works at a garment factory after her father's photo shop got burnt out in the incident. Challenging the media's distorted report of the incident as a "riot," which pits one racial group against the other, Yamashita uses Buzzworm, an African American veteran, to reread the history from the non-dominant angle: "Gonna let us know changes is in the air. Gonna let us know the real word for riots is uprisin.' Get down and preach the gospel of uprisin.'"[38] By rewriting the historical racial/ethnic conflict as an uprising (not a racial "riot"), Yamashita revises the dominant version of history and shows through her writing that racial/ethnic minorities' resistance to the systematic inequality in society is wakening.

Contrary to the U.S. promotion and celebration of diversity and cultural pluralism in the name of multiculturalism, the media's reporting of the incident as a "riot" and highlighting of interracial tensions in fact do not reflect the United States pursuing a harmonious and democratic multicultural/racial society. In *Tropic of Orange,* Yamashita's interrogation of U.S. multiculturalism—"Cultural diversity is bullshit,"[39] as expressed by Emi—leads us to question the ideological construction around the meaning of U.S. multiculturalism and its superficial understanding of racial/cultural diversity. Emi's strong aversion to cultural diversity is actually directed at the white-centered position underlying the discussion of U.S. multiculturalism. In a similar vein, Henry Giroux has aptly written: "Multiculturalism raises the question of whether people are speaking within or outside a privileged space, and whether such spaces provide the conditions for different groups to listen to each other differently in order to address how the racial economics of privilege and power work in this society."[40] Giroux points out that celebrating multicultural diversity from the white privileged position while maintaining the social and economic hierarchy along racial/ethnic differences is indeed not much different from the "condescending tolerant pluralism of liberalism's managed multiculturalism."[41]

In other words, what Yamashita challenges is U.S. multiculturalism's understanding of racial/cultural diversity at a descriptive level, since it does not reflect unequal power relations and economic disparity along race/ethnicity lines. If racially and economically marginalized minorities are still "invisible" in the discussion of cultural diversity, while focus is brought to bear only on different ethnic foods or diverse cultural products, the slogan of promoting cultural diversity is indeed instrumentalized for the interest of institutions or corporations. Yamashita's effort to use the marginalized voice to read the multicultural/racial "American" society is in this regard her way of confronting the white privileged perspective embedded in U.S. multiculturalism, and of challenging narrow perspectives on Asian American literature as a representation of ethnic differences. *Tropic of Orange* in this sense is Yamashita's redefinition of multicultural American society and her vision of critical Asian American multicultural writing.

Counteracting the Hegemonic Discourse of "America": Ruth Ozeki's *My Year of Meats*

> I am speaking from a place in the margins where I am different—where I see things differently. Speaking from margins. Speaking in resistance. I open a book. There are words on the back cover "NEVER IN THE SHADOW AGAIN," a book which suggests the possibility of speaking as liberators. Only who is speaking and who is silent. . . . Only small echoes of protest. We are re-written. We are "other." We are the margin. Who is speaking and to whom. . . . Marginality as site of resistance. Enter that space. Let us meet there. Enter that space.
>
> —bell hooks, "Marginality as Site of Resistance"

Ruth Ozeki's *My Year of Meats* (1998) is in a sense a further projection of what Karen Yamashita has shown through *Tropic of Orange.* Eschewing the existing dominant paradigms and revising the white-dominant "American" identity, Ozeki in *My Year of Meats* investigates how the media has contributed to fortifying the white-centered image of "America" and its hierarchical value system. As a way of challenging the white middle-class centered rhetoric of "America" reproduced by the media, Ozeki actively uses the media in dismantling the media-built myth of "America," and she seeks to shift the focus from the white speculative gaze towards the racially, culturally, and sexually marginalized and underrepresented groups in the United States.

Ozeki's *My Year of Meats* reveals the role of media as commerce and how the logic of capitalist expansionism penetrates into the contents of the media and how media has become a vehicle to convey the interests of sponsors or ideologies of capitalist consumer culture. In fact, the spread of U.S. capitalist culture and values through the media has been a typical way for capitalists to pursue cultural and economic infiltration. The progressive capitalist logic has been justified in the name of freedom and civilization, and mass media has contributed to reproducing the ideologies.

Ozeki's strategy to actively use the media in order to subvert the white middle-class dominant perspective of "America" and the U.S. capitalist expansionism and violence towards "others" is her way of applying resistance within the system and reflects her critical consciousness and awareness of the socioeconomic and political circumstances of U.S. society. As a Japanese American female writer, Ozeki's attempt to redirect the media angle towards the marginalized and underrepresented groups within and outside the nation is her personal and political gesture. To an interviewer's question asking if her writing is a "novel of causes," Ozeki replies: "We are leery of literature that smacks of the polemic, instructional, or prescriptive."[1] As her response implies, Ozeki is a politically conscious writer as well as an activist, and *My Year of Meats* is her personal and political manifesto reflecting her critical consciousness, her demonstration against the U.S. ambivalent rhetoric of "America," and her counter-hegemonic discourse against the U.S. capitalist culture and system.

MEDIA AS COMMERCE AND BIRACIAL IDENTITY AS A MEDIUM

Ozeki foregrounds the role of media in making the myth of "America." It is an attempt to demystify the paradoxical nature of America, the country with "landscapes hiding underground bunkers, but on the surface . . . rich with flora and fauna."[2] In a similar vein, Jean Baudrillard in *America* points out that media has played an important role in allowing people to be fascinated with an "unreal America"[3]: "The cinema and TV are America's reality."[4] Baudrillard's characterization of America as a land of contradiction—"powerful and original" yet "violent and abominable"[5]—calls attention to how media has shaped people's perception and contributed to masking the reality of "America."

In *My Year of Meats,* Ozeki through Jane Takagi-Little, a Japanese American documentarian, directly challenges the media report where the Gulf War was stated as having the fewest victims ever in the history of war. Referring to the Gulf War, Jane says, "It was January 1991, the first month of the first year of the last decade of the millennium. President Bush had just launched Desert Storm, the most massive air bombardment and land offensive since World War II. . . . Like all the parts of the Gulf War we didn't see on TV, parts that were never reported. That war was certainly a Thing That Gained by Being Painted."[6] Just as Baudrillard in an extreme manner comments that "there was no Gulf War," emphasizing the remote relation of media reports to the reality of the war, Ozeki through Jane decries the fabricated nature of media, which has become enormously influential in the postwar world, and its manipulation of ideologies, such as war, race, culture, and the image of "America" as a "savior of world democracy."

Ozeki unmasks the manner in which media has contributed to fabricating the reality of "America" and how they have obfuscated the truth from the fake, the real from the image, the documentary from the commercial, and America as a war-maker from America as a world savior. Foregrounding the role of media in the postwar periods, Ozeki further emphasizes how commercial sponsors of media corporations have been involved in message-making processes using the media for their interests and how biracial identities have been utilized in local and global markets as cultural and economic brokers mediating capitalists' interests.

In *My Year of Meats*, Jane works with Japanese crews in the New York office of the television program, *My American Wife*. The program is targeted to the Japanese audience in Japan and is sponsored by BEEF-EX, the U.S. Beef Export and Trade Syndicate. Jane finds out that she is hired for her biracial identity because a Japanese American identity becomes useful in global market contexts as a cultural/economic mediator:

> Being racially "half"—neither here nor there—I was uniquely suited to the niche I was to occupy in the television industry. . . . Although my heart was set on being a documentarian, it seems I was more useful as a go-between, a cultural pimp, selling off the vast illusion of America to a cramped population on that small string of Pacific islands.[7]

Even though she realizes that her biracial identity is utilized as a cultural broker or a transfer medium between U.S. capitalists and the media corporations in Japan, Jane takes the job because of her economic necessity.

However, contrary to the usefulness of her biracial identity in international markets, Jane realizes that her identity is still judged by people within inflexible binaries of identification. For instance, Kenji, a Japanese staff worker at the New York office, tells Jane, "You are not Japanese."[8] Jane also realizes that she is not regarded by other (white) Americans as American either. She tells about her experience with a man who questioned her identity because of her appearance:

> [A] red-faced veteran from WWII drew a bead on me and my crew, standing in line by the warming trays, our plates stacked high with flapjackets and American bacon.

> "Where [are] you from anyway?" he asked, squinting his bitter blue
> eyes at me.
> "New York," I answered.
> He shook his head and glared and wiggled a crooked finger inches
> from my face. "No, I mean where were you *born?*"
> "Quam, Minnesota," I said.
> "No, no . . . *What* are you?" He whined with frustration.
> And in a voice that was low, but shivering with demented pride, I
> told him,
> "I . . . am . . . a fucking . . . AMERICAN!"[9]

Despite being born in the United States, Jane is not identified as American
by other white Americans. In other words, racial/ethnic minorities, especially Asians, are still regarded as "aliens" in the United States. Jane's experience of not being properly defined as an American with a Japanese ethnic
background is not her personal dilemma alone. Rather, it is related to the
overall representation of what "America" is and how racial/ethnic minorities have been received in U.S. society. If "America" is represented from the
white-dominant point of view, while socially and ideologically marginalizing racial/ethnic immigrants, then the gap between the advertisement of
"America" as a country of immigrants and its actual discrimination against
racial/ethnic minorities needs to be disclosed.

Jane's identity as Japanese American, which overlaps and shares certain elements as both Japanese and American, cannot in fact be defined in
terms of either/or binaries. Like the binary thinking structure, such as Self/
Other, us/them, or American/Japanese, revealed in the dominant rhetoric
of "America," where the white middle-class is valued above racial/ethnic
immigrants in the lower classes, Jane's personal anger for not being properly identified as Japanese American in fact is related to the white-centered
hierarchical perspective and the racist discourse embedded in the rhetoric of
"America." Although the United States consists of racial/ethnic minorities
as a large part of its population, the image of "America" has still been per-
vaded with the white-dominant rhetoric, and the representation of racial/
ethnic minorities has been distorted or marginalized throughout history.

In *My Year of Meats,* the U.S. hierarchical value system is revealed
through the instruction given by BEEF-EX for the television program, *My
American Wife.* Jane finds that the instruction is reinforced by the Japanese advertising agency of BEEF-EX, and it has a white middle-class ori-
ented view of "America," one that discriminates against people of color
and people in the lower classes. Joichi Ueno, the Japanese advertising agent
of BEEF-EX, sticks to the white-centered standard of the instruction and

demands that Jane reproduce the dominant image of "America" through the program. Joichi defends himself: "I didn't make up rules. This is U.S. sponsor show and U.S. sponsor instruction."[10] Joichi, however, plays the role of a facilitator delivering the interests of BEEF-EX, and he believes in the white-centered value system that BEEF-EX embodies.

Joichi also has a firm belief in meat, thus he calls the program *My American Wife* a "documentary" rather than a commercialized cultural infiltration backed up by the U.S. meat trade syndicate. Believing in the white American-centered hierarchical belief system, Joichi urges the Japanese crews to reproduce the standard values of BEEF-EX through the program. The instruction has written the following:

DESIRABLE THINGS:

1. Attractiveness, wholesomeness, warm personality
2. Delicious meat recipe (Note: Pork and other meats is second class meats, so please remember this easy motto: "Pork is Possible, but Beef is Best!")
3. Attractive, docile husband
4. Attractive, obedient children
5. Attractive, wholesome lifestyle
6. Attractive, clean house
7. Attractive friends & neighbors
8. Exciting hobbies

UNDESIRABLE THINGS:

1. Physical imperfections
2. Obesity
3. Squalor
4. Second class peoples

***MOST IMPORTANT THING IS VALUES, WHICH MUST BE ALL-AMERICAN.[11]

The lists of "Desirable Things" and "Undesirable Things" on the instruction reveal hierarchical perspectives, placing whites and beef as superior race to colored people and pork. The Japanese television program director clarifies to Jane that the notion of "second class peoples" signifies people who do not belong to the category of "a middle-to-upper-middle class white American woman with two to three children."[12]

As the instruction "MOST IMPORTANT THING IS VALUES, WHICH MUST BE ALL-AMERICAN" indicates, the program is ideologically based on hierarchical values. The instruction is obviously discriminating against people who are economically, culturally, and racially marginalized. The instruction that BEEF-EX has provided implies that television programs have to convey the interests of commercial sponsors through the contents. BEEF-EX intends to make a "synergic" connection between the "wholesome" quality of U.S. meat and "wholesome" looking white middle-class women cooking beef for their families, which looks like an ideal picture of "America."

Following the instruction by BEEF-EX, Joichi thus demands that the Japanese television crews reproduce the white middle-class centered standards throughout the program. Although Joichi blurted out while he was intoxicated that "BEEF-EX is just a bunch of cowboys pretending to be international traders,"[13] he as the agent of BEEF-EX nevertheless plays a role in delivering the white middle-class centered U.S. capitalist values to the Japanese television audience. In other words, Joichi's belief system is more determined by his job, the economic activity. Hence Jane calls Joichi's demand to imprint the sponsor's message, "Beef is Best," on the program as a "wanton capitalist mandate."[14]

Jane opposes Joichi's hierarchical classification of race and meat, which devalues the colored people in the lower classes. The conflicting ideological stances of Jane and Joichi are clearly revealed as the program shooting develops. Despite her disagreements with Joichi and BEEF-EX's instruction, Jane is powerless in changing the white-dominant representation of "America" effected through the program. However, she does not preclude the possibility that she might have a chance to redirect the camera angle towards racially, socially, and economically marginalized people of the United States. Although she understands that her biracial identity is only utilized to mediate the interests of U.S. capitalists and the Japanese media corporations, Jane searches for a moment to challenge the dominant encoding of "America" and resists being instrumentalized as a medium of international commerce.

Through Jane, Ozeki underscores how heavily television productions rely on commercial sponsors and how the program has been manufactured to represent sponsors' interests.[15] In fact, the instruction given by BEEF-EX is intended to connect the idealized image of "America" to U.S. meat that BEEF-EX sells in international markets. In other words, through sponsoring the program *My American Wife*, BEEF-EX seeks to connect the image of U.S. beef as "authentic" and "pure" to the images of the white middle-class dominant America that are captured through the program. The com-

mercial advertisements of BEEF-EX, with its logo "Beefland," are inserted
four times in the course of the program and *My American Wife* is advertised to the Japanese audience as a "day-in-the-life type of documentary."

The program is set against the background of a vast image of "America," with a "wholesome" looking white middle-class woman as the
main character of each series. For the benefit of the program sponsor, *My
American Wife* is supposed to show the scenes of mainly white middle-
class "American" wives' cooking beef, which is the strategy proposed by
BEEF-EX as a way to "develop a powerful synergy between the commer-
cials and the documentary vehicles, in order to stimulate consumer purchase motivation."[16] BEEF-EX in a subtle manner seeks to associate the
image of "America" with scenes of white middle-class American women
cooking beef in the program and ultimately intends to promote beef consumption in Japan. In other words, the television program is being used as
a part of the BEEF-EX campaign to stimulate meat consumption in Japan
as well as "to foster among Japanese housewives a proper understanding of
the wholesomeness of U.S. meat."[17] The Japanese audience, whose source
of "America" has been mainly constructed by media such as television programs, becomes influenced by the selected images of "America" and white
middle-class "American" wives' cooking meat, which is being reproduced
by the Japanese television crews following the instruction of BEEF-EX.[18]

The ideal image of "America" and the standards of "authenticity"
and "purity" that BEEF-EX intends to connect through its sponsorship
of *My American Wife*, however, becomes suspect from the outset of the
shooting. Chosen as an "ideal" candidate for the first series of the program,
Suzie Flowers, a white middle-class woman living in Iowa with her two
children, seems to represent everything belonging to the category of "desirable things" on the lists. Set against the vast image of the Midwest America,
the first series of *My American Wife* gets started with Suzie's special recipe
of rump roast:

The Recipe of Rump roast

2 kilograms	American beef (rump roast)
1 can	Campbell's Cream of Mushroom Soup
1 package	Lipton's Powdered Onion Soup
1.5 liters	Coca-Cola (*not* Pepsi, please!)[19]

The special recipe of Rump roast that Suzie provides sounds like an advertisement of U.S. multinational commodity brands. Suzie's meat recipe in a
way represents an aspect of U.S. consumer culture. In the filming process,

Coca-Cola (*not* Pepsi), which is one of the important ingredients in Suzie's recipe, is surreptitiously replaced by Pepsi-Cola because she has run out of Coca-Cola. Suzie's Coca-Cola recipe for U.S. meat turns out to be a cultural and commercial fake. In addition, when it is revealed that Suzie's husband, Fred, had an extramarital affair, the standard of picturing a wholesome white middle-class family becomes dubious. In spite of Suzie's fake Coke meat recipe and her unwholesome marriage life, *My American Wife* ends with a kiss scene, which was taken in the beginning of the shooting of the film. Thus, the edited version of Suzie's meat cooking and her marital life are broadcast as a lovely presentation of a happy white middle-class American family, just as the image of "America" is mystified and reproduced through the media.

The scenes of white middle-class "American" wives' cooking meat on the vast scenery of America implicitly lead the Japanese audience to think of white American wives' cooking beef as an ideal "American" family life. The television program *My American Wife* becomes a cultural commodity in that the program eventually seeks for meat consumption by the audience by means of selling the images of white middle-class American wives cooking meat. *My American Wife* in this respect plays an ideological role in advertising the mystified image of "America" as well as contributing to the meat consumption of Japan.[20]

EMPOWERING "UNDESIRABLE THINGS"

Ozeki's attempt to challenge hierarchical paradigms and to demystify the connection between commercial sponsors and media production (and content) is revealed through Jane's interrogation of the white middle-class centered image of "America" and its fabricated nature in media transmission. Jane questions the instruction given by the sponsor and attempts to portray non-dominant pictures of American reality in which minority immigrants and the economically and socially marginalized are properly represented as a part of America.

Jane's effort to shoot an alternative picture of America is also her way of claiming her biracial identity as well as interrogating how media has functioned as an instrument to reinforce the white-centered perspective of "America" and its hegemonic discourse against racial/ethnic minorities in the United States. Her attempt to deliver an underrepresented reality of America is her critical gesture against the white middle-class dominant perspective of "America," its hierarchical value systems, and racist ideologies. Posing an oppositional stance towards the hegemonic discourse, Jane thus seeks to turn the conservative media angle towards the underrepresented groups of people in the United States. Jane explains:

> I was upset. I may have been glib in my pith and clumsy in my ini-
> tial dealings with the wives, but I honestly believed I had a mission.
> Not just for some girl in the next millennium, but for here and now. I
> had spent so many years, in both Japan and America, floundering in a
> miasma of misinformation about culture and race. I was determined to
> use this window into mainstream network television to *educate*. Per-
> haps it was naïve, but I believed, honestly, that I could use wives to sell
> meat in the service of a Larger Truth.[21]

Jane has attempted to capture the American reality in which racial/ethnic
minorities are part of America. Her challenging of or resisting against the
existing hegemonic discourse of "America" becomes possible through redi-
recting the perspective towards a non-dominant version of America within
the system. Thus Jane suggests to Oda, the Japanese director of the program, that they film a Mexican family, who immigrated to the United States
a long time ago and made their home in Texas. Oda, however, rejects Jane's
suggestion, taunting her with trying to make a "My Mexican Wife." Luckily, Jane's wish to shed light on the racially, ethnically, and sexually marginalized and underrepresented groups in the U. S. is finally achieved when
Oda gets shocked with antibiotic allergies after he has eaten some meat that
his "ideal" American wife cooked. Jane thus becomes a director of the program. She decides to picture underrepresented or disenfranchised groups of
people who are mostly the racially, ethnically, or sexually marginalized, and
chooses Cathy Martinez, a Mexican American woman, as her ideal candidate for *My American Wife*.

Jane's alternative vision for the program focuses more on picturing the
marginalized and underrepresented aspects of "America" rather than reproducing the existing dominant image of "America." Jane's redirection of the
focus of the program, from white middle-class women to diverse groups of
people in different racial and class categories, implies a significant change
regarding the representation of "America." Although the United States
is comprised of racially and ethnically diverse groups of people, national
identity has been narrated from the white middle-class dominant perspective, and the racial/ethnic minority has not been properly recognized as a
representative American citizen. In other words, Ozeki uses Jane to uncover
the U.S. contradictory reality in which diversity is rhetorically advertised,
yet racial/ethnic minorities are ideologically underrepresented.

Ozeki's attempt to foreground racial/ethnic minorities in the United
States draws on the Beaudroux family in Louisiana. This time, Jane pictures the scene of Mr. (not Mrs.) Beaudroux cooking Cajun style baby pork
ribs, which deviates from the standard of "desirable things" on the lists.

The unique thing about this family is that Grace and Vern Beaudroux have adopted nine children from Korea and one child from Sao Paulo besides their own two children. Through the Beaudroux family, which consists of multiracial and multiethnic groups of people, Ozeki depicts an aspect of U.S. society in which people from different racial/ethnic backgrounds live together as a family. However, like the conflicts and tension between domestic workers and minority immigrants that have occurred in the developmental process of U.S. capitalism, Jane notices that the tension and conflict arise between Joy, an adopted child from Korea and Grace's own daughter, Alison, who just gave birth to her baby:

> Alison had found Joy next to the crib in the middle of the night. It frightened her, and she had complained to Grace the next day—she didn't want her child to imprint on this image of Joy's pierced face looming over his horizon like a cloudy harvest moon. Grace told her to relax. The kids had all been older when they were adopted, so newborns were a bit of a novelty and Joy was at that age when it was natural to find infants fascinating. But privately Grace worried. Maybe it was Alison's choice of words, comparing Joy to the moon like that, but it reminded Grace of all the trouble they'd had.[22]

Ozeki uses the Beaudroux family to portray an aspect of the conflicts and tension surrounding racial/ethnic minorities in the United States. Although Grace and Vern have agreed to adopt children from racially and culturally different countries, they reveal their outlook in regarding the adopted children as the cause of the problem when dissatisfaction or complaints by their own daughter arise due to conflict with their adopted child: "No, it was Joy she [Grace] was worried about. . . . It always came back to Joy."[23]

Ozeki depicts the phenomenon of migration of racial/ethnic minorities to the United States, in the same sense that the United States is founded on labor by immigrants from different racial and cultural backgrounds. However, the way the Beaudroux family responds to Joy, in spite of their generosity and kindness in adopting the children, reflects the U.S. contradictory treatment of racial/ethnic minorities. Minority workers, who were once recruited as cheap labor, have been regarded as the cause of social and economic problems and have become excluded from the society. In addition, some children whom Grace and Vern adopted from Korea were born of relationship between Korean women and African American soldiers after the Korean War. The war has enabled U.S. soldiers to stay in Korea in the name of "national security" ever since. Most children whom the Beaudroux family adopted from Korea reflect the consequence of the social, political, and economic problems of the country, in effect an invisible colony of the United States. In other words, Ozeki through her depiction of the Beaudroux family in a way conveys a current phenomenon of immigration from the countries in which the U.S. political or economic influence is dominant.

Jane's picturing of an American reality and her approach to *My American Wife* are totally different from what Oda has captured following the white dominant standards. What Jane has projected through her camera is a non-dominant version of "America," which eschews the white-centered standards of "Americans." Through broadcasting the Martinez and the Beaudroux families, Jane has foregrounded the underrepresented image of America and has attempted to portray the reality of America in which racial/ethnic minorities are part of America and where tensions and conflicts surrounding minority immigrants have never ceased.

Jane's effort to foreground racial/ethnic minorities as a way of challenging the white-dominant values of "America," however, faces a confrontation by Joichi, the Japanese agent of BEEF-EX. The different perspectives of Jane and Joichi have been in constant conflict, as if they each represent two opposing contestants. Joichi's dominant perspective—to reproduce the white middle-class dominant view of "America"—has been challenged by Jane. Jane's attempt to subvert the hegemonic hierarchical paradigms by foregrounding the "second class people" on the lists was regarded as "undesirable" from Joichi's perspective.

Despite Jane's function as a director of the program and her disagreement with Joichi, the program comes to be guided by him, just as the tendency of the media corporations' heavy reliance on commercial sponsors implies. Thus, Joichi wields power over Jane and regularly censors the program contents, and Jane is put into a position where she has to get Joichi's permission about each episode before she starts shooting. From Joichi's perspective, Jane's shift of the camera angle from white middle-class wholesome-looking American wives to the racially, ethnically, and sexually marginalized groups of people, who are mostly the underrepresented in the United States, is regarded as an "unwholesome" portrayal of "America" deviating from the standards of "Americans." The tension between Jane and Joichi is drawn like a power struggle between the dominant and the dominated. Joichi, as the agent of BEEF-EX, has been dominating Jane and controlling the program in order to reinforce the interests of BEEF-EX. The unequal power relationships between them reflect the current tendency of media organizations' heavy dependence on commercial sponsors.

However, Jane's projection of the non-dominant aspect of "America" luckily receives a high rating from the Japanese audience, which implies a rather complicated relationship between media corporations and commercial sponsors. Joichi has asked his wife Akiko to watch the program *My American Wife* and to fill out an audience opinion form based on standards such as "general interest, educational value, authenticity, wholesomeness, availability of ingredients, and deliciousness of meat."[24] Joichi is supposed to report the responses by the audience, who are also the consumers, to his boss. Part of his job reflects a trend of multinational advertising corporations in which advertising agencies regularly check the effectiveness of their sales message. Thus Joichi asks Akiko to become an active audience as well as a meat consumer—in effect, the audience that BEEF-EX ultimately intends to seek through sponsoring the program. In order to evaluate the program, Akiko is required to cook—using the recipe offered—the meat shown on each series and to contribute to the market survey. Joichi has an ulterior motive in wanting Akiko to follow the American style of meat cooking by watching the program, because for him the way white middle-class American wives cook meat looks more "authentic." This underlying reason for asking her to learn to cook in "American" ways reflects the fact that he gives more credit to U.S. culture and values than the Japanese culture. He even wants to be called as "John Wayno" instead of Joichi Ueno saying, "Joichi is not a modern name."[25]

The tension between the couple becomes intense when Akiko gives a high rating on programs, such as the Mexican immigrant family and the Beaudroux family, which Joichi calls "unwholesome" and "unauthentic" representations of "America." From Joichi's perspective, they are racially mixed and socially inferior people, belonging to the second class, cooking the second-class meat. However, Akiko's understanding of "authenticity" and her interest in the program do not correspond to Joichi's notion of the "authentic" representation of America and its white middle-class centered standards. Whereas Joichi conforms to the existing hierarchical paradigms of race, class, and gender while following the white middle-class dominant view of America, Akiko has a more flexible way of thinking as shown through her high rating of Jane's alternative conceptualization of *My American Wife*. From Akiko's point of view, the notion of authenticity does not mean close reproduction of the white middle-class dominant version of "America," and it does not have an absolutely stable meaning either. Her responses on the Martinez and Beaudroux programs in fact dismantle unequal and hierarchical perspectives embedded in the white middle-class centered rhetoric of "America." In other words, Akiko becomes a subject who demonstrates that Jane's effort to show an alternative vision of America will have its influence on the audience. Jane's challenge of hierarchical binaries of dominant/marginalized, white/colored, and authentic/mixed is also her effort to read "America" from the non-dominant, racially, socially, and economically marginalized groups of people.

DOMESTIC DIFFERENTIATION/GLOBAL HOMOGENIZATION

Jane's attempt to capture an underrepresented aspect of America is her way of undermining hierarchical paradigms of white middle-class centered rhetoric of "America" and its discrimination against racial/ethnic minorities. Jane's realization of the contradictory rhetoric of "America" also leads her to interrogate the historical foundation of the U. S. capitalist society and the accepted principles of the country. As an example of U.S. domestic violence towards racial/ethnic minorities, Jane tells the story of Yoshihiro Hattori, a Japanese high school student who visited the United States to study as an exchange student. However, he is killed by Rodney Dwayne Peairs, a meat packer working at a supermarket. The story is that when Yoshihiro rang Peairs's bell to ask for directions, Peairs shot the boy in the chest because the boy did not listen to his yelling "freeze." Although she tells the story in a humorous tone, Jane derides the U.S. contradictory rhetoric towards racial/ethnic minorities and the media misrepresentation of minority immigrants as "criminals" or "illegal." Ozeki surmises the underlying logic behind the violence as follows:

> Hattori was killed because Peairs had a gun, and because Hattori looked different. Peairs had a gun because here in America we fancy that ours is still a frontier culture, where our homes must be defended by deadly force from people who look different. And while I'm not saying that Peairs pulled the trigger because he was a butcher, his occupation didn't surprise me. Guns, race, meat, and Manifest Destiny all collided in a single explosion of violent, dehumanized activity.[26]

Through this incident, Ozeki questions whether the emphasis on cultural diversity has really meant to understand people from different cultural and racial backgrounds, or whether it merely serves as an advertisement of "America." Although U.S. multiculturalism has promoted cultural diversity, the incident ironically reveals that the misunderstanding of racial/cultural minority groups is still pervasive. Ozeki uncovers a violent aspect of U.S. culture and how the violence is ideologically justified in the name of democracy, justice, and freedom.

Despite the United States being comprised of immigrants from different racial/ethnic backgrounds, racist ideologies and violence against people from different cultures have never ceased throughout history. The media has reproduced negative images of racial/ethnic minorities as "undesirable" to U.S. society, and restrictive immigration laws and policies have played the role of maintaining the United States as the white-dominant capitalist society.

In *My Year of Meats*, Ozeki depicts another example of a contradictory treatment of racial/ethnic minorities in the U.S. through kudzu, the plant. Ozeki uses kudzu in a metaphorical sense in order to show a repetitive pattern of recruitment and exclusion of racial/ethnic minorities in the United States. Just as many Japanese laborers were recruited as contract laborers by U.S. Sugar Planters in the 1870s, kudzu has been imported from Japan to "rehabilitate" the U.S. barren soil, because the plant has been known for its strong ability to survive tough conditions.

> It [kudzu] was introduced at the Centennial Exposition in Philadelphia in 1876, when the alien twiner was touted as "The Miracle Plant" and praised for its versatility, hardiness, and speed of growth. It could shade a bower in a matter of days and feed a herd of cows and pigs to boot. . . . In 1933 desperate to keep the South from washing away, Congress established the Soil Erosion Service, and kudzu, with its deep binding roots and its ability to reintroduce nitrogen into the soil, was seen as Dixie's savior.[27]

Although kudzu has been highly complimented for its ability to survive, more recently it has become a target for removal after it was revealed that kudzu had outgrown and engulfed indigenous plants. In a veiled metaphor for the removal of Japanese from West Coast areas through the pressure of Californians, competing for agribusiness, the Japanese experience of harsh exclusion from society is visualized through kudzu, which was once wanted for its enriching ability, but later rejected for its overgrowth. Racist ideologies of the plant as an "invasive Asian weed" have been circulating and kudzu patches are removed by the domestic people who regard it as a "life-threatening" weed that will "strangle and drown" them.

The metaphoric analogy linking kudzu to racial immigrant groups implies a cyclical pattern of acceptance and rejection with regard to racial/ethnic minorities in U.S. capitalist society and reveals the ongoing economic exploitation of racial/ethnic immigrants in the middle of an ongoing celebration of cultural diversity. Despite multiculturalism's emphasis on cultural diversity, the presence of racial/ethnic immigrants has been regarded as "threatening" and "undesirable" in society. The media has contributed to distributing the negative ideologies of racial/ethnic minorities as principal causes of social and economic problems, while hiding the fact that many capitalists favor cheap immigrant workers or undocumented immigrants for their unstable status. In fact, U.S. capitalists' exploitation of immigrant laborers as cheap and non-unionized workers has helped to sustain the system as well as to bring more profits to the capitalists. Just as the pattern of acceptance and rejection of racial/ethnic minorities has been repeated throughout the development of U.S. capitalism, ambivalent rhetoric in the U.S. about racial/ethnic immigrants has been oscillating between inclusion and exclusion of them as a part of "America."

If Ozeki has depicted the incidents of domestic violence towards racial/ethnic minorities through the cases of Hattori and kudzu, on the other hand she portrays how U.S. capitalism's outward movements have brought about a violent homogenization of other worlds under its influence, and media has become instrumentalized for its interests. Ozeki denounces the connection between U.S. capitalist expansionism and the violence embedded in the process, whereby mass media is the main means of fabricating the applicable ideologies. The media has contributed to promoting economic homogenization through cultural commodities like television programs. Mass media, which heavily relies on commercial sponsors, has become a vehicle to convey the interests of sponsors and ideologies of consumer culture and has played the leading role in distributing manipulated information or ideologies. In fact, cultural homogenization through media has become a typical way for U.S. business corporations to infiltrate world markets, especially since World War II.

Ozeki undermines the profit-oriented capitalist economic logic and interrogates the underlying connection between the U.S. capitalist expansionism and its violent infiltration to other worlds, which is justified in the name of freedom and democracy. In *My Year of Meats*, the connection between the capitalist expansionism and its justifying ideologies is depicted through BEEF-EX, the U.S. beef syndicates.[28] Jane writes: "The conflict that interests me isn't *man* versus *woman*, it's *man* versus *life*. Man's REASON, his industries and commerce, versus the entire natural world. This, to me, is the *dirty secret* hidden between the fraying covers."[29] While capturing the racially and socially marginalized groups and conflicts surrounding them in society, Jane comes to realize that the contradictory rhetoric of "America" is closely related to the economic logic of the U.S. capitalist system and its justifying logic in the name of progression and civilization. Unethical business practices, unequal power relations and inequality along race, ethnicity, sexuality, and class lines are in fact deepened in the developmental process of capitalism.

Realizing the unethical business practices that are common under the capitalist system, Jane senses a necessity to capture the unrevealed aspects of U.S. capitalism through her camera. However, Jane understands that what she attempts to shoot is directly contrary to the sponsor's interests and she will be fired after showing the program. She writes in her journal of her agony: "What am I hoping to accomplish? Am I trying to sabotage this program? I need this job. I can't afford to get fired now. On the other hand, I can't continue making the kind of programs Ueno wants, either. What am I supposed to do?"[30] Jane's concern reveals how hard it is to be politically conscious and to act beyond personal interests in the capitalist society. Despite the risk of being fired, however, Jane takes a conscious action against unfair and unethical practices in agribusiness, and she decides to capture the ugly side of U.S. capitalist society.

Ozeki's portrayal of the unethical business practice pervasive in U.S. capitalist society is depicted through Gale Dunn, a cattle feeder in Colorado. Demystifying the connection between commercial sponsors' interests and the reproduction of the message through media, Jane seeks to unmask the profit-oriented capitalist logic and unwholesome business practices underlying U.S. capitalist society and the violent capitalist infiltration of other cultures and economies. Just as Jane has emphasized, "Guns, race, meat, and Manifest Destiny all collided in single explosion of violent, dehumanized activity," unethical business practices and violence are in fact pervading every aspect of U.S. society.[31] Although the synthetic hormone DES (diethylstilbestrol) has been banned for its harmful effects, most cattle feeders, including Gale, have used DES. Jane finds out that DES is being injected into cattle, and its use has been widespread due to its economic effectiveness in spite of harmful influence on animal and human bodies:

> DES changed the face of meat in America. Using DES and other drugs, like antibiotics, farmers could process animals on an assembly line, like cars or computer chips. Open-field grazing for cattle became unnecessary and inefficient and soon gave way to confinement feedlot operations, or factory farms, where thousands upon thousands of penned cattle could be fattened at troughs. This was an economy of scale. It was happening everywhere, the wave of the future, the marriage of science and big business.[32]

The profit-oriented capitalist system has been the main reason why Gale has used DES, the "best and cheapest growth enhancer," which is illegal, yet still widespread. Gale asserts, "That's just another example of modern science comin' up with a way to kill two birds with one stone."[33] He justifies the capitalist ideology while overlooking the ethical issue involved in using DES.

While violence against nature, other cultures or people has been exercised throughout history, overall intrusive attitudes against "others" have been justified in the name of justice. "We got our own kinda justice, frontier justice," Gale asserts. The ideology of frontier justice has been upheld at the same time that U.S. capitalists have violently expanded their commodity markets beyond borders. Ozeki in the novel exemplifies the U.S.-centered globalization through the instance of Wal-Mart, the worldwide franchise market, and she further points out to how serious an extent violence has been involved in the process of U.S. capitalist expansionism. Local independent retail stores have experienced tragic changes since the monopoly-like Wal-Mart started paralyzing the diverse local scenes with its uniformity. Jane's shooting of the Bukowsky family of Polish descent shows the trauma and the tremendous conflicts that local people have gone through with Wal-Mart. Christina Bukowsky, the daughter of Elenor Bukowsky who works for Wal-Mart, is run over by a Wal-Mart delivery truck and her body is crushed. Offended by Wal-Mart's irresponsible reaction, Elenor quits her job at Wal-Mart and devotes her time to taking care of her daughter in spite of the fact that her family is financially broken. Jane's filming of the family brings attention to how badly the "exploitation of small-town America by the corporate retail giants" has changed the diverse local town cultures and has gradually paralyzed the local economy.[34]

Suzuki and Oh, the two Japanese camera crew who work with Jane, are surprised that guns are available at Wal-Mart, and they are likewise astonished by the "amplitude of America"—"the capitalist equivalent of the wide-open spaces and endless horizons of the American geographical frontier"[35]—which is displayed on the thousand shelves at Wal-Mart. Watching their faces mesmerized by the millions of products at Wal-Mart, Jane decides to shoot scenes of Wal-Mart in order to show the ambivalence of U.S. capitalist society towards the Japanese television audience:

> *This* was the heart and sole of *My American Wife!*: recreating for Japanese housewives this spectacle of raw American abundance. So we put Suzuki in a shopping cart, Betacam on his shoulder, and wheeled him up and down the endless aisles of superstores, filming *goods* to induce in our Japanese wives a state of want (as in both senses, "lack" and "desire"), because *want* is good. We panned the shelves, stacked floor to ceiling, tracked women as they filled their carts with Styrofoam trays of freezer steaks, each of which, from a Japanese housewife's perspective, would feed her entire family for several days. "Stocking up" is what our robust Americans called it, laughing nervously, because profligate abundance automatically evokes its opposite, the unspoken specter of dearth.[36]

Whereas Suzuki and Oh are amazed by the "amplitude" of Wal-Mart, Jane as a documentarian laments over the franchised markets, which eventually wipe out the indigenous culture of a society. In *My Year of Meats*, Wal-Mart or the world franchise market roams beyond geographical boundaries engulfing the local indigenous markets:

> I found that all the local business from my childhood had been extir-pated by Wal-Mart. If there is one single symbol for the demise of regional American culture, it is this superstore prototype, a huge capi-talist boot that stomped the moms and pops, like soft, damp worms, to death. . . . It is like television. But to a documentarian of American culture, Wal-Mart is a nightmare. When it comes to towns, Hope, Ala-bama, becomes the same as Hope; Wyoming, or, for that matter, Hope, Alaska, and in the end, all that remains of our pioneering aspirations are the confused and self-conscious simulacra of relic culture.[37]

Through Jane's indictment of Wal-Mart, Ozeki critically responds to the U.S. capitalization of the world through multinational brands or franchise markets, which mostly have the United States as the center.[38] Although franchised fast food restaurants and world brand commodities, which are everywhere in the world, seem to show symptoms of the decentralization of capitalist culture and economy, the United States has in fact maintained its central power and dominated the world economy since World War II.[39] Just as Wal-Mart aggressively expands its market beyond the boundary, the United States has empowered its amerocentric capitalist system to infiltrate other worlds through cultural and economic domination.

My Year of Meats in this regard is Ozeki's critical response to this monopoly-dominated capitalization of world markets and U.S. capital-ist culture, which is becoming ever more monocultural. Contrary to the promotion of cultural diversity and cultural pluralism in the name of mul-ticulturalism, domestic history proves that the United States on the one hand has accumulated profits by differentiating minority immigrants along racial/ethnic lines, while U.S. globalization of the capitalist system, on the other hand, has been achieved by homogenizing other countries under its political and economic domination. In other words, the differentiation of immigrant laborers in domestic labor markets and the homogenization of other cultures and economies into the capitalist system have worked for the development of U.S. capitalism within and outside the nation. U.S. mul-ticulturalism's celebration of cultural diversity in a way has disguised the oppressive and totalitarian nature of U.S. capitalism that has gradually ter-ritorialized the world under its umbrella. Indeed, the two seemingly different processes—differentiation and homogenization—manifest their participation in an interconnected world capitalist system and show how they have worked for the development of the U.S. capitalism within and outside the nation and how U.S. multiculturalism has become an ideological narrative of capitalism.[40]

In this respect, to celebrate diversity and difference in the United States is simply to veil "continuity in oppression and inequality" by generating a "simulated plurality."[41] Ozeki's challenging of U.S. capitalism's tendency to homogenize other cultures and economies is thus her interrogation of the ongoing discussion of U. S. multiculturalism's promotion of cultural diversity, which is rhetorically floating in the air, yet unrecognizable in reality.

Conclusion
Multiculturalism, or an International Marketing of U.S. Capitalism

Do I have to explain why "exotic" pisses me off, and "not exotic" pisses me off? They've got us in a bag, which we aren't punching our way out of. To be exotic or to be not-exotic is not a question about Americans or about humans.

—Maxine Hong Kingston, *Tripmaster Monkey*

In contemporary racism, cultural difference (ethnicism) serves as the most efficacious modality of racializing interpellation.

—E. San Juan Jr., *Beyond Postcolonial Theory*

Multiculturalism has, over the years, acquired aspects of a holy cow for many, a cash cow for some. Both are dangerous creatures. Standing on consecrated ground, they resent being disturbed and, when challenged, are inclined to bite. But a society that wishes to remain healthy and to grow must, from time to time, stare the holy cows down; it must probe and question them, and decide on their merits and usefulness. To fail to do so is to atrophy.

—Neil Bissoondath, *Selling Illusions*

It is evident that the current discussion of U.S. multiculturalism, which acknowledges the cultural and ethnic differences of racial/ethnic groups, has downplayed the manner in which ethnic groups' differences are utilized with respect to the division of labor, wage differentiation, or unequal opportunities. It appears that inequality based on race, gender, and nationality is still persistent in society, and the economic mechanism that has oppressed and exploited racial/ethnic minorities has not been properly brought out in the discussion of U.S. multiculturalism. Symptomatic of this position is the

descriptive level of cultural diversity and difference highlighted in politically acquiescent Asian American multicultural literary works.

Stereotyping a racial/ethnic group implies an unequal power relationship active in the socioeconomic structure of the society. So, like the writers
I have been elucidating, I have attempted to dismantle the myth of Asian
Americans as a "model minority." The goal of such a process is an attempt
to articulate and thus undermine the existing dominant power structure, so
that Asian Americans might begin to consciously react to the discrimination
they have experienced against their race and ethnicity in the United States.
Just as earlier Asian laborers (especially Chinese), who were racially pre-
defined as coolies, were favorably received by white employers as "models"
for labor-striking domestic workers, the "middlemen" position into which
Asian immigrants have been situated in the U.S. economy has not changed
across time. In the twentieth century, the ambivalent position of Asian immigrants as middlemen was continued in the interests of having a "self-serving model minority" as compared to African Americans and Chicanos/Latin
Americans. Although Asian immigrants were "yellow proletariat" in the
nineteenth century and are now called a "middle-class model minority," the
ambivalent position in which they have been situated as middlemen—either
as a "union-dissolving force" or as a "model" for other racial minorities—
has not been much changed in terms of how they have served U.S. capitalist
development and ideological stabilization while supplying their cheap labor.

In fact, with the preference-based Immigration Act of 1965, the
migration of skilled professionals in the area of science and technology has
increased. Despite many Asian immigrants still struggling within the boundary of their ethnic communities and despite their social and economic marginalization in society, the "successful" myth of Asian Americans and Asian
immigrants as a "model minority" has become widespread. The irony is that
many Asian immigrants have taken the label as a compliment without questioning the underlying ideological implications and without acknowledging
how the label has been ideologically applied to sustain the system's stability.

In some ways, Asians' passive conformity to the dominant economic
demands has prevented them from involving themselves in social and
political issues and also fostered socio-political indifference and conserva-
tism. In addition, descendents of Asian immigrants and many recent immigrants with professional skills were relatively quick to secure themselves
in the United States and showed a strong tendency to assimilate to the
white privileged dominant culture. They have tried to "whiten" themselves
through economic success. Some recent Asian immigrants, who are more
like the upper class in their country of origin, tend to have a conservative
perspective on U.S. politics and history in general while believing that the

development of science and technology, the areas where they are mostly clustered, will bring democracy and a better future to the society.

Neo-conservative perspectives that some Asian immigrants have taken on social progressivism have also helped to cover the racial discrimination and economic exploitation that are, I believe, inherent in the U.S. economic structure. However, what these Asian Americans failed to realize is that in spite of their investment, an emphasis on education as a way to achieve economic upward mobility does not get an equal return in terms of wage and opportunity compared to other white skilled workers. No matter how highly they are qualified, there seems to be a certain limit that racial/ethnic minorities cannot rise above as a group. This structural hierarchy and power inequality cannot be resolved at individual levels, and the ideology of meritocracy-based individual achievement has masked the unequal power structure of the society.

Despite Asian Americans being touted as a "good example" to white "American" society, structural inequality along racial/ethnic lines has continued, and they are still politically disenfranchised. In this regard, Harry Kitano alerts Asian Americans to the need to self-consciously react to their internalization of the ideology and the stereotype tagged on them:

> Our drive for acceptance has really been to follow the cues of the dominant society, and they have told us that to be successful you have to be quiet and humble and those other characteristics. If we really believe that that's the way we can become successful, then one can become rather pessimistic about the future of our group because that means that we have been "conned" or that we have "conned" ourselves almost completely into taking a second-class role.[1]

In other words, politically acquiescent Asian Americans have "conned" themselves into seeing only economic success as the way of elevating their status and have internalized the conforming attitude while contributing to the media-spread image of Asian Americans as a "model minority." What they should be aware of is that the stereotypical image of Asian Americans merely replicates the ambivalent yet conservative role of Asian Americans as system supporting "middlemen"—a "non-threatening" group, yet still a "disempowered" minority.

If "successful" Asian Americans are a "model" to the society, then they should be regarded as representative citizens. However, the label "minority" implies that no matter how long Asian immigrants have lived in the United States, the projection of Asian Americans as racial/cultural "others" has not changed, and the white dominant perspective remains. As one of the critical

Asian American writers, Kingston thus asks Asian Americans to challenge their continuing stereotyping as "exotic," "unassimilable," or a "model minority," and urges them to question the imposed image:

> The job of the characters they let you play gets upgraded from criminal or servant to semi-professional, and you're fooled that we're doing better. Just because you get to wear a nurse's uniform rather than a Suzie Wong dress doesn't mean you're getting anywhere nearer to the heart of that soap. You're not the ones they tune in every day to weep over. We need to be part of the daily love life of the country, to be shown and loved continuously until we're not inscrutable anymore.[2]

As Kingston points out, Asian immigrants themselves need to confront the stereotype of Asian Americans that is shaped for the dominant interests of society. Asian Americans need to critically examine how they have been culturally and economically exploited in the United States and they also need to extricate themselves from the mystified ideology of a "model minority" which they have internalized.

The media-fostered image of Asian Americans as a "successful minority" due to their ethnically distinctive behavior closely corresponds to the institutionalized version of multiculturalism in that it tends to shift attention from racial contexts to cultural terrains that mask racial/ethnic tensions in society. U.S. multiculturalism has undergone criticism for its underlying white dominant assumptions that leave the color of white ethnic culture invisible in the background while marginalizing and essentializing racially and ethnically different groups as racial "minorities." In the same manner that the politically neutralizing tendency of U.S. multiculturalism fails to address the unequal power structure and interactions of race and class, politically acquiescent Asian Americans' uncritical reception of the myth of "model minority" has prevented them from seeing how they have been ambivalently situated as middlemen in the U.S. economy, and how their mediate position has contributed to stratification among other racial and ethnic minorities, ultimately causing interracial tensions and conflicts. U.S. multiculturalism's politically disengaging attitude can be seen to reverberate in the manner in which the Asian American "success" myths mask or de-politicize the structured racism.

The instrumentally utilized yet internally marginalized position of Asian Americans is in some ways replicated in U.S. academic curricula, as seen through the status of Asian American Studies (or Asian American literature within American Literature), which were created after the critical racial movement of the 1960s. Since the late 1960s, Asian Americans have attempted to claim a lawful right as representative citizens in the United States. Asian American Studies emerged in educational reform efforts following the request of Asian Americans for acknowledgement of their history and culture in the curriculum, and it was certainly an accomplishment that Asian American studies emerged as a legitimate program in U.S. academia.[3] In spite of its origin as a "protest against the existing education structure" that excluded Asian Americans, however, Asian American Studies was received as "a form of *compensatory* education that would add to but not substantially alter the institution."[4] In other words, despite Asian American Studies being established in U.S. universities as an acquisition of a critical space to delineate specific Asian American experience, the difference in terms of race and ethnicity, regardless of intentions, has been utilized to the point that it fosters an essentialized difference and has ironically contributed to demarcating the line between dominant whites and colored "others." Much like the hierarchy maintained between domestic whites and racial/ethnic minorities in socioeconomic, cultural, and institutional levels, Asian American Studies within U.S. academic institutions has fallen into circumstances defined by unequal relations between the dominant and marginalized. Yamashita in an interview with Ryuta Imafuku comments about the remarkable reversion of the Asian American movement of the 1960s towards a static ethnic program:

> The Asian American Movement was a vital and exciting time that happened along with the Black Power Movement and other movements in the United States. These movements changed the picture of the academy's response to ethnicity in the United States. Yet, these movements have been eaten up by the academy in the sense that ethnic studies programs created in this period now have to produce the same kind of work that they were perhaps rebelling against.[5]

As Karen Yamashita has indicated, Asian American studies are now reproducing hierarchical relations between the dominant/marginalized and the core/periphery as well as the "same old ideologies" that reinforce the stereotype of Asians as "essentially" different "ethnic others." In addition, Asian American Studies programs rarely exist as an independent discipline, and they have been put into a vulnerable position when universities experience financial cutbacks.[6]

Interestingly, the period when Asian American Studies received attention and became considered a part of academic disciplines coincides with the discussion of multiculturalism emerging in the late 1980s.[7] Although the University of California at Berkeley first initiated ethnic studies as a "distinct discipline-based department" in 1969, it was actually in the 1980s that the ethnic studies department started to develop its program with a "more comprehensive vision," and in the case of the University of California, San Diego, it was not until 1990 that the ethnic studies department was approved.[8] Even after Asian American Studies (or Asian American literature) was regarded as a part of academic programs, it has remained marginal nonetheless.[9]

Just as conservative multiculturalists reduce ethnic groups to add-ons to the dominant culture, so was Asian American Studies regarded in U.S. academia as a "luxury that universities could not afford" or as an add-on to the existing curriculum, an add-on that could be removed depending on circumstances.[10] Despite academia's slogan of promoting multiculturalism and diversity, the peripheral status of Asian American Studies within universities reflects the ongoing unequal power relations in society and the politically disenfranchised and socially marginalized status of Asian Americans.

In effect, Asian American Studies (or Asian American literature within American Literature) in U.S. academic institutions assumes the form, borrowing from Graham Huggan, of "institutionalization of marginality" and "comes with the seal of academic approval that may only help to commodify it."[11] In other words, racial/ethnic differences not only become racialized in U.S. labor markets but also commodified in cultural texts and institutions in the sense that cultural diversity is merely advertised for the system or institution's sake. Thus it happens that "minority" immigrants have been exploited along lines of race and ethnicity and they also become commodified as "cultural others" in late capitalist market. David Li notes how racial/ethnic differences become exploited in market-oriented economic society:

> When multicultural artifacts and products are turned containable, collectible, and consumable, capitalism's subordination of racialized and gendered labor in the economic realm also becomes invisible. Difference begins to justify the identification of different commodities with different markets and becomes a vehicle for maintaining social distinctions.[12]

In other words, U.S. multiculturalism's emphasis on ethnic differences has successfully packaged the racial/ethnic "others" as cultural commodities, which is a form of "cultural representation under late capitalism."[13] Much as U.S. multiculturalism's emphasis on the ethnicity paradigm has contributed to reading race as "one more difference on the all-American continuum of ethnic diversity," current multiculturalism is superficial in its diversity commitment, because it still bears a white superior perspective behind the ideology.[14] Li in this regard has written:

> Strangely enough, the evocation of difference does not represent a true departure of identitarian thought but rather its privatization. Although the discourse of difference has ransacked the essentialization of identity beyond repair, the prevalent reference to difference as a thing in and by itself, as a floating signifier or a transcendent category of endless enumeration, leads to the reproduction of essentialism in and through categorical isolation and individuation.[15]

Identity politics, which offered racial/ethnic "minority" groups a voice to reconstruct their own "collective identities," became problematized, because of a tendency to produce a "politics of assertion that is both essentialist and separatist," reproducing "the very problem it was attacking."[16] Although an understanding of identity and difference was promoted as a way to challenge the white-dominant hegemony, a cultural politics of identity and difference, such as multiculturalism, was utilized to the point that it fosters an essentialized difference, and it was elaborated without an accompanying "social politics of justice and equality."[17] U.S. multiculturalism has its limits in terms of interrogating the structural inequality practiced against racial/ethnic minorities. In fact, no matter what difference in race and culture is celebrated, the value of difference cannot be fully appreciated without issuing a challenge to unequal power relations in society.

The currently prevalent discussion of multiculturalism is thus nothing but a refashioned, conservative ideology that disguises the ongoing differentiation against racially and culturally different groups of people. Stanley Fish, in this regard, uses the name "Boutique multiculturalism" for the currently dominant, yet superficial level of understanding diversity. According to Fish,

> Boutique multiculturalism is the multiculturalism of ethnic restaurants, weekend festivals, and . . . is characterized by its superficial or cosmetic relationship to the objects of its affection. Boutique multiculturalists admire or appreciate or enjoy or sympathize with or (at the very least) "recognize the legitimacy of" the traditions of cultures other than their own; but boutique multiculturalists will always stop short of approving other cultures at a point where some value at their center generates an act that offends against the canons of civilized decency as they have been either declared or assumed.[18]

In fact, the U.S. slogan of multiculturalism has not been much different from the advertising of ethnic festivals at government or institutional levels. Fish's labeling of the current multiculturalist conception as boutique multiculturalism may be regarded as an accurate diagnosis of conservative U.S. multiculturalism: it is racially invisible yet culturally commodified.

The conservative aspect revealed in the current multiculturalism leads us to question why the United States should have promoted multiculturalism and diversity in the late 1980s at the academic institutional and corporate levels. The frequent use of the term in universities, according to Kandice Chuh and Karen Shimakawa, reflects a symptom of "academic globalization"—a process that tracks and keeps pace with socioeconomic changes and globalization.[19] If Fish has pointed out a (neo)conservative stance that current U.S. multiculturalism takes towards racial/ethnic "minority" groups, Chuh and Shimakawa interpret the emergence of multiculturalism as an academic response to U.S. globalization.[20] Their emphasis on multiculturalism as "the effect of globalization" suggests the possibility of reading Asian American Studies in relation to the changing socioeconomic phenomenon.

In effect, promotion of multicultural diversity in universities and inclusion of Asian American Studies as a curriculum are both an academic extension of U.S. globalizing capitalism. Thus Li interprets the "legitimization of Asian American texts as the influence of market multiculturalism" and connects Asian American studies in its relationship with U.S. corporate and State policy.[21] In a similar vein, Masao Miyoshi links U.S. promotion of multiculturalism and the reformed Immigration Act of 1965 to the development of U.S. capitalism and U.S. demand for skilled professionals beyond the national boundary. In fact, U.S. multinational corporations (MNC) and transnational corporations (TNC) developed in the late 1960s and the 1970s respectively.[22] The number of people from different national and ethnic backgrounds—especially Asians after the Immigration Act of 1965—has increased as a consequence of U.S.-centered globalization and transnational trade. Miyoshi reads U.S. multiracial/cultural society as a product of capitalist development and interprets the superficial level of "color-blind" multiculturalism as an aspect of corporate management of diverse groups of people. He has written:

> First, TNCs will increasingly require from all workers loyalty to the corporate identity rather than to their own national identities. Second, employees of various nationalities and ethnicities must be able to communicate with each other. In that sense, TNCs are at least *officially and superficially trained to be color-blind and multicultural.* Despite

the persistent recurrence of violent racist events in the United States, its immigration regulations were radically changed in 1965 to reject the ethnically defined quota system set out by the 1952 McCarran-Walter Act. In the revised immigration Reform and Control Act of 1986 and the November 1990 reform bill, priorities are given to skills rather than ethnicities. TNCs, especially, are allowed to claim a quota from the category of 40,000 aliens with special abilities in addition to the general category of skilled experts and professionals.[23] (My emphasis added)

Miyoshi points out that the reformed immigration acts of 1965, 1986, and 1990 were made as a part of the attempt by the U.S. to bring in skilled laborers. The composition of U.S. multiracial/cultural society is thus a systematic consequence of capitalist development, and U.S. promotion of multiculturalism at institutional and corporate levels is an ideological justification of U.S. capitalism. Miyoshi even asserts that U.S. multiculturalism has been promoted to "disguise transnational corporatism," and it serves as another floating advertisement of "America" while mystifying the contradictory U.S. capitalist reality.[24]

Historically, U.S. capitalists' utilization of minority laborers from various countries by means of recruitment, colonization, or Bracero contract was intended to achieve more profit by hiring at a cheaper wage and by splitting and stratifying the labor market along race and ethnicity lines. Recruitment of laborers who are different in language, culture, and nation was in fact sought actively by U.S. capitalists. Despite differences being utilized to justify hierarchized wages and labor divisions throughout capitalist history, what the U.S. advertises through multiculturalism is an ideological make-over for the structural inequality practiced against racial/ethnic minorities and an euphemistic way of manipulating diverse groups of people. Thus San Juan Jr. asserts that multiculturalism is a renewed "racial politics of cultural difference" in that U.S. capitalism "refunctions racism through the ideology of differential culturalism."[25]

Cultural differences in fact cannot be fully appreciated without achieving equality at socioeconomic levels. Current U.S. multiculturalism's lack of commitment to democratizing diversity at structural levels has been revealed through various incidents. For instance, Asian American students' high percentage of undergraduate enrollment at the University of California at Berkeley was used as an example to question the usefulness of affirmative action in the 1980s. In an extension, George W. Bush made a speech on January 15, 2003 regarding the University of Michigan's decision whether to treat race as a criterion for an admission decision. He used "diversity" to criticize affirmative action on the grounds that any "quota" based on race or ethnicity is "unconstitutional." Bush has announced:

> I strongly support diversity of all kinds, including racial diversity, in higher education, but the method used by the University of Michigan to achieve this important goal is fundamentally flawed. . . . America is a diverse country, racially, economically and ethnically. And our institutions of higher education should reflect our diversity. . . . Yet quota system that use race to include or exclude people from higher education and the opportunities it offers are divisive, unfair and impossible to square with the Constitution. . . . Recent history has proven that diversity can be achieved without using quotas.[26]

If the United States has pursued diversity in order to appreciate difference and to rectify the systematic inequality practiced against racial/ethnic minorities, then affirmative action, which was legalized to include minority groups at institutional and corporate levels, should be protected. However, the term diversity was ironically borrowed to justify the past discrimination in this context, while being used as a backdrop for the invalidation of affirmative action.

Despite U.S. multiracial/cultural society being advertised as an ideal of "America," racial/cultural diversity within the nation has been threatened in many ways. Amid the advertising of cultural diversity in the United States, media misrepresentations of immigrant workers as the source of "high employment" and "rising cost of social welfare" have never ceased, nor have the INS's periodic crusades on undocumented immigrants. U.S. capitalists' demands for cheap labor by means of "backdoor policies" or "legal loopholes" have continued nonetheless, and inconsistent immigration policies have created more "illegal visa-overstayers," who later are forced to work underground without being protected. This reveals an aspect of ongoing U.S. contradictory treatments of racial/ethnic minorities and the conservative perspective of viewing non-white groups as "threatening" to the society. In other words, U.S. alleged promotion of multiculturalism and diversity is not intended to speak for racial/ethnic minorities. As shown through ambivalent treatment of minorities, U.S. multiculturalism as a justifying ideology of U.S. capitalism reproduces unchanged the same dubious attitude toward racial/ethnic minorities.

Rather than being applied to democratize the systematic inequality in society, multiculturalism has been an ideological gesture to the globalizing U.S. multi/transnational economy, and at corporate levels the idea of multiculturalism was encouraged in order to recruit and manage diverse groups of people in a more effective way. In fact, U.S. promotion of diversity in universities and in the workforce plays a role as an ideological narrative revealing the direct influence of corporate market economy, which is becoming a "pervasive nature" in late capitalist society.[27]

U.S. society has been continuously working along according to white dominant paradigms, while placing "multiculturalism" as an updated advertisement to promote the image of "America." Despite the gesture of embracing racial/ethnic minorities, current U.S. multiculturalism's lack of commitment to democratizing diversity at structural levels has not been challenged. In addition, in deference to the dominant discussion of multiculturalism there has been an abandonment of the critical voice that interrogates unequal power relations in society and demands equality at structural levels. Thus, it becomes an important task for critical Asian Americans to seek after a more democratic multicultural condition that contests inequality against racial/ethnic minorities and to create a counter-hegemonic discourse, challenging the ongoing discrimination and exploitation against race and ethnicity. Although each Asian immigrant group has its own different experience and faced racial discrimination in unique ways, the treatment of most Asian immigrants in the U.S. labor market can be described in reference to a common collective experience. In order to develop a sense of critical consciousness and belonging as a legitimate citizen in the United States, Asian Americans should not view themselves merely as a unit among ethnic groups. Rather, Asian Americans need to form a strong solidarity as a unified racial identity beyond ethnic differences.

In rejection of their status as an obedient mass and economically utilized yet socio-politically disenfranchised minority, Asian Americans need to stand up as "critical citizens," challenging U.S. ambivalent attitudes affecting minorities and immigrants within the nation. While remembering the socioeconomic discrimination practiced against minorities, critical Asian Americans—writers, critics, and activists—should politically engage through questioning the U.S. politics of difference, and they should critically react to the ongoing discrimination and exploitation practiced against people who are racially and ethnically different from the dominant white groups in society, which is the very opposite approach to that posed by institutionalized and commercialized trends of current U.S. multiculturalism.

Notes

NOTES TO THE INTRODUCTION

1. Christopher Newfield and Avery Gordon, "Multiculturalism's Unfinished Business," in *Mapping Multiculturalism*, eds. Avery Gordon and Christopher Newfield (London and Minneapolis: University of Minnesota Press, 1996), 96.
2. Ibid., 89.
3. Angela Davis, "Gender, Class, and Multiculturalism," in *Mapping Multiculturalism*, eds. Avery Gordon and Christopher Newfield (London and Minneapolis: University of Minnesota Press, 1997), 44.
4. This is especially true of immigrants from Southeast Asia. Since the fall of Saigon in 1975, sizable populations of Asians from Vietnam, Cambodia, and Lao immigrated to the United States. These so-called refugee-turned-immigrants from Southeast Asia were underrepresented even among the Asian communities in the United States.
5. Henry Giroux, "The Politics of Insurgent Multiculturalism in the Era of the Los Angeles Uprising," in *Critical Multiculturalism*, eds. Barry Kanpol and Peter McLaren (London and Westport: Bergin & Garvey, 1995), 117.
6. Edward San Juan, Jr., *Racial Formations /Critical Transformations* (New York: Humanity Books, 1992), 106.
7. Peter McLaren, "White Terror and Oppositional Agency: Towards a Critical Multiculturalism," in *Multiculturalism*, ed. D.T. Goldberg (Cambridge: Blackwell, 1994), 49–50.
8. Ibid., 51.
9. Ibid., 53.

NOTES TO PART ONE

1. Leith Mullings, "Ethnicity and Stratification in the Urban United States," in *Racism and The Denial of Human Rights: Beyond Ethnicity*, eds. Marvin Berlowitz and Ronald Edari (Minneapolis: MEP Publications, 1984), 23.

2. Chan, Jeffery Paul, Frank Chin, Lawson Fusao Inada, and Shawn Wong, *THE BIG AIIIEEEEE!* : *An Anthology of Chinese American and Japanese American Literature* (New York: A Meridian Book, 1990), xi-xii.
3. Ibid., xii.
4. Ibid., xii.
5. Thus Chan and the others point out: "One measure of the success of white racism is the silence of the minority race and the amount of white energy necessary to maintain or increase that silence." See Jeffery Paul Chan, Frank Chin, Lawson Fusao Inada, and Shawn Wong, *Aiiieeeee!: An Anthology of Asian-American Writers* (Washington D.C.: Howard UP, 1974), xxvi.
6. Chan and the others write: "The stereotype operated as a model of behavior. . . . The stereotype operates most efficiently and economically when the vehicle of the stereotype, the medium of its perpetuation, and the subject race to be controlled are all one. . . . The race poses no threat to white supremacy. It is now a guardian of white supremacy, dependent on it and grateful to it." Ibid., xxvii.

NOTES TO CHAPTER ONE

1. Kitty Calavita, *U.S. immigration Law and the Control of Labor, 1820–1924* (New York and London: Academic Press INC, 1984), 4.
2. Ibid., 76.
3. Edna Bonacich, "Asian Labor in the Development of California and Hawaii," in *Labor Immigration Under Capitalism,* eds. Lucie Cheng and Edna Bonacich (Berkeley: University of California Press, 1984), 159.
4. Ronald Takaki, *Iron Cages* (New York: Alfred Knopf, 1979), 234.
5. Bonacich 159.
6. Robert Lee, *Orientals: Asian Americans in Popular Culture* (Philadelphia: Temple University Press, 1999), 56–66.
7. "Coolie" is from "kuli," a Tamil word meaning hired, unskilled laborer. It was first used by Chinese merchants residing in Southeast Asia to refer to local aboriginals and imported laborers from India. Historically, many Chinese laborers who were taken to Peru and Cuba worked as coolies in the 1870s. Although the Chinese migration to the United States was enacted voluntarily, I use the term "coolie" to refer to cheap immigrant laborers whose labor was utilized by capitalists. See Ronald Takaki, *Strangers From A Different Shore* (Boston, New York, and London: Little Brown, 1989), 36.
8. Lee 58.
9. Ibid., 59.
10. Ibid., 67.
11. Ibid., 64–65.
12. Maxine Hong Kingston, *China Men* (New York: Vintage Books, 1980), 140.
13. "In 1870, some 250 Chinese workers who had been recruited to work on the Houston and Texas Central Railroad filed suit against the railroad for breach of contract when the railroad failed to live up to its promises. Hundreds of Chinese who had been brought in to build the Alabama and

Chattanooga Railroad were among the workers who seized the company's cars and equipment when that company went bankrupt in an attempt to enforce their demands for back wages." See Robert Lee's *Orientals* 65.

14. Peter Kwong, *The New Chinatown* (New York: Hill and Wang, 1987), 11–12.
15. Bill Hing, *To Be An American* (London and New York: New York University Press, 1997), 21.
16. Ibid., 27.
17. Calavita 1. Lisa Lowe also points out that immigration exclusion acts and naturalization laws have been not only a means of regulating the terms of the citizen but have also defined Asians as "culturally and racially other." See Lisa Lowe, *Immigrant Acts* (Durham and London: Duke University Press, 1996), 5.
18. Ibid., 236.
19. Lucie Cheng and Philip Yang, "The 'Model Minority' Deconstructed," in *Contemporary Asian America*, eds. Min Zhou and James Gatewood (New York and London: New York University Press, 2000), 476.
20. *U.S. News and World Report,* "Success Story of One Minority Group in U.S," December 26, 1966, in *Roots: An Asian American Reader,* eds. Amy Tachiki, Eddie Wong, Franklin Odo, and Buck Wong (California: The Regents of the University of California, 1971), 6.
21. The label Asian Americans was coined in the late 1960s in order to refer to the collective body of Asian immigrants in the United States.
22. Morrison Wong, "Post-1965 Asian Immigrants," in *The History and Immigration of Asian Americans,* ed. Franklin Ng (New York and London: Garland Publishing Inc, 1998), 154.
23. John Liu and Lucie Cheng, "Pacific Rim Development and the Duality of Post-1965 Asian Immigration to the United States," in *The New Asian Immigration in Los Angeles and Global Restructuring,* eds. Paul Ong, Edna Bonacich, and Lucie Cheng (Philadelphia: Temple University Press, 1994), 75.
24. Ibid., 75.
25. The migration of unskilled laborers also occurred, but relatively small numbers immigrated. Unskilled workers could migrate to the United States with a valid work visa. However, occupations were limited to the labor in short supply in U.S. labor markets. Strict visa interviews and income review made it hard for low-income workers to legally immigrate to the United States. In many cases, immigrants who came under family reunification took menial jobs, while skilled workers, professionals, or students became permanent residents once they were hired in the areas where U.S. labor was in short supply.
26. Liu and Cheng 95.
27. Cheng and Yang 474.
28. Ibid., 475.
29. Ibid., 476.
30. Michael Scott-Blair, "Ethnic Imbalance Shifts at UC," *San Diego Union,* December 11, 1986. Requoted in Takaki's *Strangers From A Different Shore* 498.
31. Viet Thanh Nguyen, *Race and Resistance* (New York and Oxford: Oxford University Press, 2002), 146.

32. Richard Appelbaum, "Multiculturalism and Flexibility," in *Mapping Multiculturalism,* eds. Avery Gordon and Christopher Newfield (London and Minneapolis: University of Minnesota Press, 1996), 313.

NOTES TO CHAPTER TWO

1. Graham Huggan, *The Postcolonial Exotic: Marketing the Margins* (London and New York: Routledge, 2001), 35.
2. Huggan notes that the exotic is the "perfect term to describe the domesticating process through which commodities are taken from the margins and reabsorbed into mainstream culture." Ibid., 22.
3. Neil Bissoondath, *Selling Illusions* (New York: Penguin Books, 1994), 214.
4. Huggan 14.
5. Ibid., vii–ix.
6. Elaine Kim, *Asian American Literature: An Introduction to the Writings and Their Social Context* (Philadelphia: Temple University Press, 1982), 60.
7. Xiao-huang Yin, *Chinese American Literature Since the 1850s* (Urbana and Chicago: University of Illinois Press, 2000), 135.
8. Sandra Dijkstra, Amy Tan' literary agent, set an initial contract with G. P. Putnam's Sons for *The Joy Luck Club* at $50,000. In addition to her first contract, Tan received $1.2 million from Vintage for the paperback rights for *The Joy Luck Club.* See details in E.D. Huntley's *Amy Tan: A Critical Companion* (Westport, Connecticut & London: Greenwood Press, 1998), 10–12.
9. Ibid., 29. See also Chin et al., xxii.
10. Amy Ling, "Chinese American Women Writers," in *Maxine Hong Kingston's The Woman Warrior: A Casebook,* ed. Sau-ling Cynthia Wong (New York and Oxford: Oxford University Press, 1999), 143.
11. Yin 154.
12. Kim 71.
13. Ibid., 71.
14. Ibid., 59.
15. Judy Yung provides the historical circumstance in which Wong's several essays were favorably received by the mainstream readership:

> "After the Japanese attacked Pearl Harbor, thirty-nine shipyards sprang up in the Bay area, ready and eager to build the Liberty Cargo carriers and large tankers needed for America to win the war. Because of the labor shortage as well as federal guidelines against discrimination in hiring, all of the major shipyards were willing to hire racial minorities and women. Chinese Americans, who had long been excluded from industrial employment but who were now seen in a more favorable light by white America, were among those recruited" (*Unbound Voices* 473).

Due to a turn of historical events, most Chinese Americans who used to be confined in Chinatown were then able to work outside Chinatown.

Having worked as a private secretary at Marinship, Wong wrote: "Chinese at Marinship are each in his or her way working out their answer to Japanese aggression by producing ships which will mean their homeland's liberation" (*Unbound Voices* 474). Although the historical situation and U.S. demand for laborers were the main reasons for Chinese Americans being favorably received in the labor market, Wong seems to regard this change as society's "benevolent" gesture towards Chinese Americans. See Judy Yung, *Unbound Voices: A Documentary History of Chinese Women In San Francisco* (London and Berkeley: University of California Press, 1999), 473–74.

16. E. D. Huntley has written, "Jade Snow Wong's *Fifth Chinese Daughter* describes an ethnic world in which existing stereotypes are confirmed and sanitized. Her book provided the predominantly white readership of the war years with a picture of Chinese American life that was both intriguing and easy to accept as genuine because it conformed to the mythical China that already existed in the popular American consciousness." See Huntley's *Amy Tan: A Critical Companion* 24.

17. Yin 149.

18. Ibid., 135.

19. Ibid., 139.

20. Ibid., 140.

21. Ibid., 139.

22. Karen Su, "Jade Snow Wong's Badge of Distinction in the 1990s," *Hitting Critical Mass: A Journal of Asian American Cultural Criticism* 2.1 (1994): 13.

23. Jade Snow Wong, *Fifth Chinese Daughter* (1950) (Seattle and London: University of Washington Press, 1989), Introduction to the 1989 edition, viii.

24. The ideological image of Chinese Americans as a "loyal minority" is also reinforced through the speech by Mr. Wong, Jade Snow's father, on the importance of self-reliance, hard work, and high aspiration towards education as well as his argument against people's tendencies to rely on government relief. Mr. Wong says,

> "But it is my desire not to apply for relief, even though we may need it. I do not want my children to experience getting anything without first working for it, for they may become selfish, and a selfish person can wander the world over and still starve for lack of food. Selfishness often starts with a spirit of dependency; therefore I want my children to learn to cope with the world, and to understand that they get what they want only after working for it" (*Fifth Chinese Daughter* 54).

What Mr. Wong states exactly corresponds to the ideology of a "model minority" that does not depend on government welfare checks and tries to overcome poverty by working hard and saving money towards education. Wong's narrative of a "model minority," and her downplaying of racial discrimination in this regard, reflect that she has conformed to the ideological stereotypes of Chinese immigrants.

25. Su 12–13.
26. Ibid., 14.
27. Ibid., 18.
28. Wong 114.
29. Ibid., 189.
30. Ibid., 244–45.
31. Huggan in this respect aptly notes, "Exoticism effectively hides the power relations behind these labels, allowing the dominant culture to attribute value to the margins while continuing to define them in its own self-privileging terms." Huggan 24.
32. Ibid., 43.
33. Patricia Chu, *Assimilating Asians* (Durham and London: Duke University Press, 2000), 167.
34. "The novels and autobiographies by the Chinese-born writers are moving accounts of women's firsthand experience of war. They describe the refugees waiting day and night outdoors for trains to take them from threatened cities; boats so crammed that people perished in the crush or were drowned trying to get aboard; the devastation of Japanese incendiary bombs flattening building, creating giant craters and walls of flame, leaving bloody corpses and charred bones." Ling 143.
35. Amy Tan, *The Joy Luck Club* (New York: Ivy Books, 1989), 141.
36. Ibid., 129.
37. Ibid., 3.
38. Ibid., 7.
39. Ibid., 10.
40. Ibid., 18.
41. Ibid., 16–17.
42. Ibid., 319.
43. Ibid., 319.
44. Chu 141.
45. Ibid., 150.
46. "As a freelance writer, Amy Tan produced a wide array of projects for several major corporations: training manuals for AT& T sales personnel who were assigned to promote 'Reach Out America,' business proposals for national consulting firms, and even a book for IBM, *Telecommunications and You,* aimed at systems engineers and company CEOs who were involved with the growing telecommunications field. She also worked on projects for Bank of America and Pacific Bell." See Huntley 7.
47. Huggan xiv.
48. Huntley 23.
49. Ibid., 23.
50. Huggan 155.
51. Sau-ling Cynthia Wong, "Autobiography as Guided Chinatown Tour?" in *Maxine Hong Kingston's The Woman Warrior: A Casebook,* ed. Sau-ling Cynthia Wong (New York and Oxford: Oxford University Press, 1999), 30.
52. Jeff Chan, "Chairman of SF State Asian American Studies, Attacks Review," *The San Francisco Journal,* May 4 (1977): 6.

53. Susan Brownmiller, "Talks with Maxine Hong Kingston, Author of The Woman Warrior," in *Maxine Hong Kingston's The Woman Warrior: A Casebook,* ed. Sau-ling Cynthia Wong (New York and Oxford: Oxford University Press, 1999), 175.

54. King-Kok Cheung, "The Woman Warrior versus the Chinaman Pacific: Must a Chinese American Critic Choose between Feminism and Heroism," in *Maxine Hong Kingston's The Woman Warrior: A Casebook,* ed. Sau-ling Cynthia Wong (New York and Oxford: Oxford University Press, 1999), 124.

55. Benjamin Tong, "Critic of Admirer Sees Dumb Racist," *The San Francisco Journal,* May 11 (1977): 6.

56. Maxine Hong Kingston, "Cultural Mis-readings by American Reviewers," in *Asian and Western Writers in Dialogue: New Cultural Identities,* ed. Guy Amirthanayagam (London: Macmillan, 1988), 55.

57. Ibid., 57.

58. Kingston in *China Men* makes it clear that it was Yueh Fei not Fa Mu Lan who had carved words on his back. Kingston tells in a more direct manner that the reason she changed the original legend of the warrior in *The Woman Warrior* is not because of her ignorance of traditional Chinese legends. Rather it was an artistic strategy designed to deliver her unauthentic Chinese identity, where the original cannot be distinguished from the transformation, or the real from the fake. See Kingston's *China Men* 56.

59. The part where Fa Mu Lan gives birth to a baby in the midst of battle and returns to her army is, in my view, unrealistically depicted. Kingston might have expected readers to realize the unrealistically absurd story as a sort of parody. In some ways, what Kingston tries to convey through parodying the Chinese legend is related to what the narrator feels about her parents, who demand that she grow like an authentic Chinese girl in America. The way her parents raise her to be like an authentic Chinese girl in the United States sounds as if the narrator hears stories or Chinese legends outside their social and historical contexts. The reason she changes or deviates from the Chinese legends that her mother has told is most easily understood in this context.

60. Kingston's *The Woman Warrior* 48 and 53.

61. Sheng-Mei Ma, *The Deathly Embrace: Orientalism and Asian American Identity* (London and Minneapolis: University of Minnesota Press, 2000), xvii.

62. Katheryn Fong. Reprinted in Wong's "Autobiography as Guided Chinatown Tour?" 30–31.

63. Huggan x.

64. Ibid., xi.

65. Wong 6.

66. Maxine Hong Kingston, *The Woman Warrior: Memoirs of A Girlhood Among Ghosts* (1976) (New York: Vintage, 1989), 7.

67. The way Kingston approaches "No Name Woman" is considerably different from how Tan has depicted the stories of An-mei's mother in that Kingston tries to convey the stories of the Chinese women from their perspectives and provides the socio-economic and historical contexts.

68. Kingston, *The Woman Warrior* 3.

69. David Leiwei Li, *Imagining The Nation: Asian American Literature and Cultural Consent* (Stanford: Stanford University Press, 1998), 61.

70. Kingston, *China Men* (New York: Vintage Books, 1980), 67.

71. From 1882 until 1943, the Chinese Exclusion Act prohibited all Chinese except teachers, students, and diplomats from entering the United States. The first time when Chinese women were allowed to immigrate was through a provision in the Immigration Act of 1952.

72. Kingston, *The Woman Warrior* 96.

73. Ibid., 126–27.

74. Ibid., 152–53.

75. Brownmiller 178.

76. Kingston, *The Woman Warrior* 184.

77. Wong 31.

78. The term, "measuring silences," was used by Pierre Macherey. According to Macherey, "what is important in a work is what it does not say." This is not the same as "what it refuses to say." Rather it is closer to the meaning, "what it cannot say." Reprinted in Gayatri Chakravorty Spivak, "Can the Subaltern Speak?" in *Marxism and the Interpretation of Culture,* eds. Cary Nelson and Lawrence Grossberg (Urbana: University of Illinois Press, 1988), 286.

NOTES TO PART TWO

1. Lisa Lowe, *Immigrant Acts* (Durham and London: Duke University Press), 16.

2. Ibid., 25–26.

3. Karl Marx. *Capital* (1894) Vol 3. Ch. 14, section 5, 1909, requoted in Michael Barratt Brown. *The Economics of Imperialism* (Baltimore: Penguin Books, 1974), 60.

4. Lowe 161.

5. Tim Libretti, "America Is In The Heart," in *A Resource Guide to Asian American Literature,* eds. Sau-ling Cynthia Wong and Stephen Sumida (New York: The Modern Language Association of America, 2001), 22.

NOTES TO CHAPTER THREE

1. Displacement or migration of people from one place to another has occurred throughout the world. The distinctive characteristic in modern movement is that it is the migration of labor, not the migration of people, which occurs in the developmental process of modern capitalism. See The Santa Cruz Collective on Labor Migration, "The Global Migration of Labor and Capital," in *U.S. Capitalism in Crisis* (New York: URPE, 1978), 108–09.

2. Edna Bonacich, "A Theory of Ethnic Antagonism: The Split Labor Market," *American Sociological Review* 37 (1972): 549.

3. Unlike Chinese and Filipino immigrants, Japanese immigrants could bring their family with them, which was a part of the provision between the Japanese government and the United States. However, the Gentlemen's Act of 1907 eventually stopped the flow of migration of Japanese workers.

4. Bulosan 5.

5. Ibid., 23–24.

6. Americans managed the Department of Education in the Philippines. The teachers, so-called "solider-teachers" supplied from the U.S. army used English as the language for its instruction. U.S. education of Filipinos has consciously or unconsciously inculcated Filipinos with an idolatry for "American" values and an American way of life. Regarding the education that Filipinos received under U.S. sovereignty, Schirmer and Schalom point out that it was a "convenient instrument" for colonial policy, because U.S. soldier-teachers emphasized an "American" ideal of liberty and freedom and the lives of American heroes through the education. See Daniel Schirmer and Stephen Rosskamm Schalom, eds, *The Philippines Reader* (Boston: South End Press, 1987), 45–46.

7. Bulosan 20–21.

8. Carey McWilliams, *Brothers Under the Skin* (1942) (Boston: Little, Brown and Company, 1964), 229–32.

9. Edward San Juan, Jr., *Reading the West/Writing the East* (New York: Peter Lang, 1992), 137.

10. Bulosan 63.

11. Edward San Juan Jr. *On Becoming Filipino: Selected Writings of Carlos Bulosan* (Philadelphia: Temple University Press, 1995), 173.

12. Ibid., 125.

13. Lucie Cheng and Edna Bonacich, *Labor Immigration Under Capitalism* (Berkeley: University of California Press, 1984), 2.

14. Paul Sweezy explains that the utilization of the reserve army of labor, which is mostly composed of nationally and racially oppressed groups in the United States, is to make the wage level more competitive in domestic labor markets: "The industrial reserve army, during the periods of stagnation and average prosperity, weighs down the active labor army; during the periods of overproduction and paroxysm, it holds its pretensions in check. Relative surplus population is therefore the pivot upon which the law of demand and supply of labor works. It confines the field of action of this law within the limits absolutely convenient to the activity of exploitation and to the domination of capital." See Paul M. Sweezy, *The Theory of Capitalist Development* (New York and London: Modern Reader Paperbacks, 1970), 87.

15. Bulosan 101–02.

16. As a way of keeping wages down, various restrictive methods were employed in the process of recruiting laborers. Cheng and Bonacich summarize three major ways that employers or national bourgeoisie have suppressed minority workers and kept their wage low: 1) Be "selective" about who can enter. For instance, immigrant law can select for "able bodied young men while excluding all dependent populations, such as women, children, the elderly, the sick, and paupers"; 2) Keep immigrant workers in

a "special legal category." As noncitizens, immigrant workers are vulnerable to being shipped home at the slightest provocation; 3) Bind workers to contracts while they are still in their home country. "The workers may be unaware that the provisions of the contracts they sign are highly unfavorable when compared with conditions of other workers in the country of immigration. Yet on arrival they are subject to threats of legal action if they break their contracts." See Cheng and Bonacich 32–33.

17. Bulosan 158.
18. Ibid., 146.
19. "Exclusion movements generally occur when the majority of a cheaper labor group resides outside a given territory but desires to enter it. The exclusion movement tries to prevent the physical presence of cheaper labor in the employment area, thereby preserving a non-split, higher priced labor market." See Bonacich's "A Theory of Ethnic Antagonism: The Split Labor Market," 553–54.
20. Ronald Takaki, *Strangers from a Different Shore* (Boston, New York, and London: Little Brown, 1989), 319.
21. Bulosan 143–44.
22. Ibid., 180 and 222.
23. Ibid., 195.
24. This act promised independence to the Philippines on July 4, 1946, after a 10 year-transition (the Commonwealth Period) and contained a provision for limiting the Filipino migration to fifty persons a year. The Tydings-McDuffie Act was the subject of varied interpretations. It was first interpreted as a relief to the Philippines government and nationalists, because the Philippines could have their own sovereignty. However, independence of the Philippines was a nominal liberation from the United States in that the colonial trade pattern between the countries was still maintained until 1946 and even after. See Stephen Rosskamm Shalom, *The United States and the Philippines* (Philadelphia: A Publication of the Institute for the Study of Human Issues, 1981), xv.
25. With the passage of the Tydings-McDuffie Act, the most seriously damaged group was Filipino laborers in the United States, because their status was changed from U.S. nationals to aliens. They could not get any social benefits even when they became impoverished and suffered from social and economic exclusion. The real purpose of the law, as McWilliams points out, was the "Filipino exclusion." McWilliams notes the underlying reason behind the Tydings-McDuffie Act as follows: "Originally allowed to enter the United States as 'cheap labor,' Filipino farm laborers had completed their 'brief but strenuous period of service to American capital': they were no longer needed because of the availability of Mexican labor and no longer wanted because of their labor militancy." McWilliams, "Exit the Filipino," Reprinted in Takaki 333.
26. Bulosan 186.
27. Ibid., 312.
28. Ibid., 311–12.
29. Fae Myenne Ng, *Bone* (New York: HarperPerennial, 1993), 145.

30. Ibid., 148.
31. Ibid., 40.
32. Ibid., 50.
33. Ibid., 103.
34. Ibid., 58.
35. Ibid., 56.
36. Ibid., 56
37. Ibid., 61.
38. Ibid., 17.
39. Sau-ling Cynthia Wong relates food imageries to the issues of necessity and poverty, which indirectly indicate the socioeconomic status of immigrants in Chinatown. *Reading Asian America Literature* (Princeton: Princeton University Press, 1993), 28–34.
40. Ng 44.
41. Ibid., 45.
42. Ibid., 45.
43. Ibid., 148.
44. Richard Appelbaum notes that the recent change in the garment industry reflects an ongoing restructuring of U.S. capitalism shifting around the availability of a cheap labor within and outside the nation. He explains, "Beginning a generation ago, high and rising costs in the unionized apparel industry of the northern United States began to drive factories out of the region, first to the south, then to Mexico and the Caribbean, to Asia, to the world—and today back home to Los Angeles, where an abundance of impoverished immigrants from Mexico and Central America render long-distance subcontracting in search of cheap labor less necessary." See Appelbaum, "Multiculturalism and Flexibility," in *Mapping Multiculturalism*, eds. Avery Gordon and Christopher Newfield (London and Minneapolis: University of Minnesota Press, 1966), 309.
45. Ng 174.
46. Referring to the ongoing restructuring of capitalism as the "racialized feminization of labor," Lowe notes that the global restructuring of capitalism has "gendered" and "racialized" minority workers. Asian immigrant women, especially after 1965, have been conveniently exploited as a low-paid and labor-intensive workforce. U.S. restructuring of capitalism has continuously shifted around the availability of cheap(er) laborers. Asian and Latino women since the 1980s have become a "cheaper and flexible" labor force: "[T]he proletarianization of Asian and Latina immigrant women is a current instance of the contradiction between the globalization of the economy and the political needs of the nation-state; it takes place in conjunction with a gendered international division of labor that makes use of third world and racialized immigrant women as a more "flexible," "casual," "docile" workforce." See Lowe 160.
47. Ng 163.
48. Ibid., 176–77.
49. The subcontracting system has brought advantages to manufacturers by providing them with flexibility. The reason manufacturers prefer subcontracting

is that they no longer need to worry about labor organization, because contractors, who are mostly immigrants, hire documented or undocumented
workers at a cheap price. Subcontracting eventually helps manufacturers to
bring the cost down and be competitive in garment industries. Although
contractors and laborers are employees of the manufacturer, under the subcontracting system contractors become workers' "immediate oppressors"
and become a target of "interethnic hostility." See Edna Bonacich, "Asian
in the Garment Industry," in *The New Asian Immigration in Los Angeles
and Global Restructuring,* eds. Paul Ong, Edna Bonacich, and Lucie Cheng
(Philadelphia: Temple University Press, 1994), 158.
50. Ng 178.
51. Ibid., 139.

NOTES TO CHAPTER FOUR

1. Claudia Sadowiski-Smith, "The U.S.-Mexico Borderlands Write Back:
   Cross-Cultural Transnationalism in Contemporary U.S. Women of Color
   Fiction," *Arizona Quarterly* 57.1 (2001): 101.
2. King-Kok Cheung, *An Interethnic Companion to Asian American Literature* (Cambridge: Cambridge University Press, 1997), 19.
3. Jean Vengua Gier and Carla Alicia Tejeda, "An Interview with Karen
   Yamashita," at http://social.chass.ncsu.edu/jouvert/v2i2/yamashi.htm.
4. Lisa Lowe has stated: "Despite the usual assumption that Asians immigrate
   from stable, continuous, "traditional" cultures, most of the post-1965
   Asian immigrants come from societies already disrupted by colonialism and
   distorted by the upheavals of neocolonial capitalism and war." See Lowe's
   Immigrant Act 16.
5. Ibid., 16–21.
6. Karen Tei Yamashita, *Tropic of Orange* (Minneapolis: Coffee House Press,
   1997), 15.
7. Ibid., 17–18.
8. Ibid., 17.
9. Ibid., 19.
10. Ibid., 23.
11. Ibid., 128.
12. Ibid., 126.
13. Ibid., 203–04.
14. Molly Wallace, "Tropics of Globalization: Reading The New North Amer-
    ica," *Symploke* 9.2 (2001): 155.
15. Ibid., 155.
16. Yamashita 110.
17. The Japanese were "unwanted competitors" in California's agricultural busi-
    ness, and the racial discrimination against Japanese immigrants was prac-
    ticed as a means of eliminating economic competition in the agribusiness
    area. Carey McWilliams explains, "[I]t is certainly true that special-inter-
    est groups were active in exerting pressure for mass evacuation. The ship-
    per-grower interests in Washington were opposed to mass evacuation. . . .

But the California shipper-grower interests were definitely in favor of mass evacuation and for admittedly selfish reasons. Shortly after December 7, the Shipper-Grower Association of Salinas sent Mr. Austin E. Anson to Washington to lobby for mass evacuation. 'We're charged with wanting to get rid of the Japs for selfish reasons,' said Mr. Anson. 'We might as well be honest. We do. It's a question of whether the white man lives on the Pacific Coast or the brown men. They came into this valley to work, and they stayed to take over.'" (*Saturday Evening Post,* May 9, 1942. requoted in McWilliams's *Prejudice* 127). See Carey McWilliams, *Prejudice* (Boston: Little Brown, 1945), 126–27.

18. A character in *No-No Boy* argues, "I got it all figured out. Economics, that's what. I hear this guy from the stars, the general of your army that cleaned the Japs off the coast, got a million bucks for the job. All this bull about us being security risks and saboteurs and Shinto freaks, that's for the birds and the dumbheads. The only way it figures is the money angle." See John Okada, *No-No Boy* (Seattle: University of Washington Press, 1957), 32–33.

19. Yamashita 158.

20. Ibid., 37.

21. Ibid., 237–38.

22. Rafaela directly questions the media's ideological distortion practiced against racial/ethnic minorities: "Nobody respects our work. Say we cost money. Live on welfare. It's a lie. We pay taxes." Ibid., 80.

23. Helene Hayes, *U.S. Immigration Policy and the Undocumented* (Westport: Praeger, 2001), 21.

24. Contrary to the media misrepresentation of the undocumented immigrants as "welfare-dependents," most of them do not apply for welfare or tax refund (although they pay taxes), because they are afraid of being caught. Because of their "illegal" status, which was increased by restrictive immigration law, most undocumented immigrants work at far less than the minimum wage. The existence of "illegal" immigrants was in effect utilized to lower the overall wage level in U.S. society. Ibid., 9–26.

25. Yamashita 141.

26. Hayes 27–38.

27. Gloria Anzaldua, *Borderland/La Frontera* (San Francisco: Aunt Lute Books, 1987), 33.

28. Yamashita in her interview says that her character, Arcangel, is very much influenced by the work of Guillermo Gomez-Pena:

> "Arcangel is based on Guillermo Gomez-Pena. In fact, he says things that Gomez-Pena says. The first time I saw and watched him perform and read his work, I was fascinated. I've had this sensation that, in Los Angeles, he has been, in some ways, rejected—I'm not sure. Arcangel is a literary interpretation of Pena. Arcangel's performance is grotesque, freakish, yet Christ-like, accounting for 500 years of history in the Americas. He's also like Neruda, who, through his great poem, *Canto General,* expresses all of Latin America. He takes the poetry, and also the political conscience and history across the border." See Gier and Tejeda. 3.

29. Yamashita 47.
30. Ibid., 131.
31. Ibid., 132.
32. North American Free Trade Agreement (NAFTA), which the United States and Mexican governments agreed to in 1994, has eroded tariffs between Mexico and the United States. Thus U.S. goods could penetrate into Mexico more freely than ever, and it eventually made U.S.-centered capitalist expansionism much easier. It is clear that the Mexican economy has become more dependent on and dominated by the United States, and the Mexican markets have become saturated with U.S. commodities. The upper-class conspiracy of the two governments, which eventually destroyed Mexicans' economic means to survive in their indigenous society, basically serves capitalist interests.
33. Yamashita 147.
34. Claudia Sadowski-Smith comments that Mexico's economic dependency on the U.S. has deepened through NAFTA:

    "Whereas Mexico (and partly Canada) have opened their economies and lifted restriction on foreign investment under pressure from NAFTA, the United States continues to undermine the kinds of neo-liberal ideologies to which it ostensibly subscribes by instituting various forms of market protectionism for its own economy, while relentlessly bombarding other nations, including its neighbors, with the doctrines of free trade."

    See *Globalization on the Line: Culture, Capital, and Citizenship at U.S. Borders*, ed. Claudia Sadowski-Smith (New York: Palgrave, 2002), 8.
35. Yamashita 259–60.
36. Michael Murashige, "Karen Tei Yamashita: interview with Murashige," in *Words Matter*, ed. King-Kok Cheung (Honolulu: University of Hawaii Press, 2000), 330–31.
37. Gier and Tejeda 8.
38. Yamashita 216.
39. Ibid., 128.
40. Henry Giroux, "The Politics of Insurgent Multiculturalism in the Era of the Los Angeles Uprising" in *Critical Multiculturalism*, eds. Barry Kanpol and Peter McLaren (Westport: Bergin & Garvey, 1995), 108.
41. David Theo Goldberg, *Multiculturalism: A Critical Reader* (Cambridge: Blackwell, 1994), 26.

NOTES TO CHAPTER FIVE

1. Penguin Books, "A Conversation with Ruth Ozeki," in *My Year of Meats* (New York: Penguin Books, 1998), 8.
2. Ruth Ozeki, *My Year of Meats* (New York: Penguin Books, 1998), 247.
3. Jean Baudrillard, *America* (London and New York: Verso, 1988), 102.
4. Ibid., 104.
5. Ibid., 88.

6. Ozeki 7 and 360.
7. Ibid., 9.
8. Ibid., 228.
9. Ibid., 11.
10. Ibid., 119.
11. Ibid., 11–12.
12. Ibid., 13.
13. Ibid., 194.
14. Ibid., 167.
15. Herbert Schiller suggests that the corporate business system has utilized media for its own objectives, with media becoming a vehicle for spreading the consumer culture throughout the world, and he points out that the "tendency of media commercialization intensifies as the multinationals extend their economic activity." See Herbert Schiller, *National Sovereignty and International Communication* (Norwood: Ablex Publishers, 1979), 25.
16. Ozeki 41.
17. Ibid., 10.
18. Cees J. Hamelink provides an explanation for the advertising trend and its impact on audience perception. Hamelink states that the most important channels that advertising agencies use are mass media. It has become popular for transnational advertising agencies to insert their advertising between television programs as a strategy to expand their international markets in a persuasive way. He further emphasizes that advertising influences the audience perception in the long run because the audience comes to identify with the culture and values of the country, which is mainly America: "An important impact of imported advertising campaigns is that values in the U.S. are reproduced in other countries." See Cees Hamelink, *Cultural Autonomy in Global Communications* (New York and London: Longman, 1983), 16.
19. Ozeki 19.
20. Schiller points out the connection between the globalization of U.S. commodity markets and the role of media as its conveyor, and he comments that commercialization of the mass media has been dominant since the television program is heavily relying on commercial sponsors, and media industry in a way has fallen into a status of "commercial culture producing business." Schiller 25.
21. Ozeki 27.
22. Ibid., 82.
23. Ibid., 83.
24. Ibid., 21.
25. Ibid., 21.
26. Ibid., 89.
27. Ibid., 76.
28. Schiller points out that sponsoring television programs has been strategically used to infiltrate foreign economy. Schiller 30.
29. Ozeki 154.
30. Ibid., 210.

31. Ibid., 89.
32. Ibid., 125.
33. Ibid., 262.
34. Ibid., 135.
35. Ibid., 35.
36. Ibid., 35.
37. Ibid., 56–57.
38. Despite multi/transnational corporations and franchise markets becoming dominant since World War II, the center of power has not been scattered to other territories. Anthony Brewer interprets the postwar global expansion of capitalism as U.S.-centered imperialism (Brewer 265–67). Michael Hardt and Antonio Negri agree that the postwar phenomenon of globalization is more America-based. However, their argument is based on the definition of imperialism as a "political form." Whereas Brewer's argument on globalizing capitalist production is understood within the economic realm, Hardt and Negri regard the globalization of U.S. capitalist markets as the "decline of the political sovereignty of nation-states" and the "inability to regulate economic and cultural exchange," and they name it "Empire" (Hardt and Negri xi). Their interpretation of "Empire" is different from "totalitarian imperialism" in that Empire established "no territorial center of power" and it does not rely on fixed boundaries or barriers: "It is a *decentered* and *deterritorializing* apparatus of rule that progressively incorporates the entire global realm within its open, expanding frontiers" (Ibid., xii). For them, the capitalized Empire is the "period of a new peaceful phase of capitalism that goes beyond the violent conflicts of imperialism." In contrast to Hardt and Negri's assertion that "imperialism is over," I would rather argue that the postwar capitalist development is centering around the United States, and it is an extension of capitalist imperialism, which is more economically based. See Anthony Brewer, *Marxist Theories of Imperialism: A Critical Survey* (London and New York: Routledge, 1989), 265–67. Also, see Michael Hardt and Antonio Negri, *Empire* (Cambridge: Harvard University Press, 2000), xi-xii.
39. Gilles Deleuze and Felix Guattari in *A Thousand Plateaus* celebrate the "no centeredness" of the interaction between "deterritorialization and territorialization." See Gilles Deleuze and Felix Guattari, *A Thousand Plateaus: Capitalism and Schizophrenia*, Tr. Brian Massumi (Minneapolis: University of Minnesota Press, 1987), 431–37.
40. The U.S. homogenization of the world under its capitalist system while discriminating against racial minorities within the nation reveals a "totalizing" tendency of U.S. capitalism. To my thinking, this continuous capitalist development through homogenizing others-outside while differentiating others-within is another form of totalization, which reveals the manifest destiny of U.S. capitalism.
41. Ziauddin Sardar, *Postmodernism and the Other* (London and Chicago: Pluto Press, 1998), 38.

NOTES TO THE CONCLUSION

1. Harry Kitano, "Interview," in *Roots: An Asian American Reader*, ed. Amy Tachiki (Los Angeles: Continental Graphics, 1971), 84.
2. Maxine Hong Kingston, *Tripmaster Monkey: His Fake Book* (New York: Vintage International, 1990), 310.
3. Ibid., 157–65.
4. Shirley Hune, "Area Studies and Asian American Studies: Comparing Origins, Missions, and Frameworks," in *Asian Americans: Comparative and Global Perspectives*, eds. Shirley Hune, Hyung-chan Kim, Stephen Fugita, and Amy Ling (Pullman: Washington State University Press, 1991), 1.
5. See Karen Tei Yamashita and Ryuta Imafuku, "The Latitude of the Fiction Writer: A Dialogue," at http://www.cafecreole.net/archipelago/Karen-Dialogue.html.
6. Goldberg points out, "Faculty hired in the name of the multicultural or the demands of diversity are at once ghettoized and terrorized by traditional disciplinary determinations and considerations. While the appeal of programs lies in their critical independence and transdisciplinarity, their vulnerability is revealed most immediately in times of economic retrenchment. Least institutionalized in the academy, they are most prone to deficit reduction; last created, first decimated." See "Introduction: Multicultural Conditions," in Goldberg's *Multiculturalism*. 8.
7. David Li, *Imagining the Nation* (Stanford: Stanford University Press, 1998), 186.
8. Ramon Gutierrez, "Ethnic Studies: Its Evolution," in *Multiculturalism*, ed. David Theo Goldberg (Oxford and Cambridge: Blackwell, 1994), 162–64.
9. Kandice Chuh, "Imaginary Borders," in *Orientations*, eds. Kandice Chuh and Karen Shimakawa (Durham and London: Duke University Press), 278.
10. Amy Ling, "The State of Asian American Studies in Wisconsin," in *Reviewing Asian America*, eds. Wendy Ng, Soo-Young Chin, James Moy, and Gary Okihiro (Pullman: Washington State University Press, 1995), 195–96. Also, see Chuh 277–78.
11. Huggan 23.
12. Li 195.
13. Huggan 14.
14. Paula Rothenberg, "The Construction, Deconstruction, and Reconstruction of Difference," *Hypatia* 5 (1990): 46.
15. Li 193.
16. Henry Giroux, "Resisting Difference: Cultural Studies and the Discourse of Critical Pedagogy," in *Cultural Studies*, eds. Lawrence Grossberg, Cary Nelson, and Paula Treicher (New York: Routledge, 1992), 208.
17. Nancy Fraser, "Equality, Difference, and Radical Democracy," in *Radical Democracy*, ed. David Trend (London: Routledge, 1996), 207.
18. Stanley Fish, "Boutique Multiculturalism or Why Liberals Are Incapable of Thinking about Hate Speech," *Critical Inquiry* 23 (1997): 378.

19. Kandice Chuh and Karen Shimakawa, eds. *Orientations* (Durham and London: Duke University Press, 2001), 6.

20. Chuh and Shimakawa note, "Globalization, after all, works in multiple directions; while much critical work examines the effects of that process 'elsewhere' (or on our conceptions of that "elsewhere"), we end by considering these effects within Americans studies, which takes as its object that from which, ostensibly, 'global' effects flow—but on which the effects of globalization have rarely been taken seriously." Ibid., 11.

21. Li 186.

22. Masao Miyoshi. "Borderless World? From Colonialism to Transnationalism and the Decline of the Nation-State," *Critical Inquiry* 19 (1993): 726–51.

23. Ibid., 741.

24. Ibid., 751.

25. San Juan 11.

26. George W. Bush, "Affirmative action quotas unconstitutional." January 15, 2003. See the article at www.cnn.com/2003/ALLPOLITICS/01/15/bush.aa.transcript

27. Mike Alexander Pozo, "An Educator's Reflections on the Crisis in Education and Democracy in the United States: An Interview with Henry A. Giroux," See the interview at www.axisoflogic.com.

Bibliography

Anzaldua, Gloria. *Borderland/La Frontera*. San Francisco: Aunt Lute Books, 1987.

Appelbaum, Richard. "Multiculturalism and Flexibility." *Mapping Multiculturalism*. Eds. Avery Gordon and Christopher Newfield. London and Minneapolis: University of Minnesota Press, 1966.

Baudrillard, Jean. *America*. London and New York: Verso, 1988.

Bissoondath, Neil. *Selling Illusions*. New York: Penguin Books, 1994.

Bonacich, Edna. "Asian in the Garment Industry." *The New Asian Immigration in Los Angeles and Global Restructuring*. Eds. Paul Ong, Edna Bonacich, and Lucie Cheng. Philadelphia: Temple University Press, 1994.

———. "Asian Labor in the Development of California and Hawaii." *Labor Immigration Under Capitalism*. Eds. Lucie Cheng and Edna Bonacich. Berkeley: University of California Press, 1984.

———. "A Theory of Ethnic Antagonism: The Split Labor Market." *American Sociological Review* 37 (1972): 549–54.

Brewer, Anthony. *Marxist Theories of Imperialism: A Critical Survey*. London and New York: Routledge, 1989.

Brown, Barratt. *The Economics of Imperialism*. Baltimore: Penguin Books, 1974.

Brownmiller, Susan. "Talks with Maxine Hong Kingston, Author of *The Woman Warrior*." *Maxine Hong Kingston's The Woman Warrior: A Casebook*. Ed. Sau-ling Cynthia Wong. New York and Oxford: Oxford University Press, 1999.

Bulosan, Carlos. *America Is In the Heart: A Personal History*, 1946. Seattle and London: University of Washington Press, 2000.

Bush, George W. "Affirmative action quotas unconstitutional." January 15, 2003. www.cnn.com/2003/ALLPOLITICS/01/15/bush.aa.transcript.

Calavita, Kitty. *U.S. Immigration Law and the Control of Labor, 1820–1924*. New York and London: Academic Press INC, 1984.

Chan, Jeffery. "Chairman of SF State Asian American Studies, Attacks Review." *The San Francisco Journal*. May 4, 1977.

Chan, Jeffery Paul, Frank Chin, Lawson Fusao Inada, and Shawn Wong. *THE BIG AIIIEEEEE! : An Anthology of Chinese American and Japanese American Literature*. New York: A Meridian Book, 1990.

Cheng, Lucie and Edna Bonacich. *Labor Immigration Under Capitalism*. Berkeley: University of California Press, 1984.

Cheng, Lucie and Philip Yang, "The 'Model Minority' Deconstructed." *Contemporary Asian America*. Eds. Min Zhou and James Gatewood. New York and London: New York University Press, 2000.

Cheung, King-Kok. *An Interethnic Companion to Asian American Literature*. Cambridge: Cambridge University Press, 1997.

———. "The Woman Warrior versus the Chinaman Pacific: Must a Chinese American Critic Choose between Feminism and Heroism." *Maxine Hong Kingston's The Woman Warrior: A Casebook*. Ed. Sau-ling Cynthia Wong. New York and Oxford: Oxford University Press, 1999.

Chin, Frank, Jeffery Paul Chan, Lawson Fusao Inada, and Shawn Hsu Wong. *Aiiieeeee!: An Anthology of Asian-American Writers*. Washington D.C.: Howard University Press, 1974.

Chu, Patricia. *Assimilating Asians*. Durham and London: Duke University Press, 2000.

Chuh, Kandice and Karen Shimakawa, Eds. *Orientations*. Durham and London: Duke University Press, 2001.

Davis, Angela. "Gender, Class, and Multiculturalism." *Mapping Multiculturalism*. Eds. Avery Gordon and Christopher Newfield. London and Minneapolis: University of Minnesota Press, 1997.

Deleuze, Gilles and Felix Guattari. *A Thousand Plateaus: Capitalism and Schizophrenia*. Tr. Brian Massumi. Minneapolis: University of Minnesota Press, 1987.

Fish, Stanley. "Boutique Multiculturalism or Why Liberals Are Incapable of Thinking about Hate Speech." *Critical Inquiry* 23 (1997): 378–95.

Fraser, Nancy. "Equality, Difference, and Radical Democracy." *RadicalDemocracy*. Ed. David Trend. London: Routledge, 1996.

Gier, Jean Vengua and Carla Alicia Tejeda. "An Interview with Karen Yamashita." http://social.chass.ncsu.edu/jouvert/v2i2/yamashi.htm. 1.

Giroux, Henry. "Resisting Difference: Cultural Studies and the Discourse of Critical Pedagogy." *Cultural Studies*. Eds. Lawrence Grossberg, Cary Nelson, and Paula Treicher. New York: Routledge, 1992.

———. "The Politics of Insurgent Multiculturalism in the Era of the Los Angeles Uprising." *Critical Multiculturalism*. Eds. Barry Kanpol and Peter McLaren. London and Westport: Bergin & Garvey, 1995.

Goldberg, David Theo. *Multiculturalism: A Critical Reader*. Cambridge: Blackwell, 1994.

Gutierrez, Ramon, "Ethnic Studies: Its Evolution." *Multiculturalism*. Ed. David Theo Goldberg. Oxford and Cambridge: Blackwell, 1994.

Hamelink, Cees. *Cultural Autonomy in Global Communications*. New York and London: Longman, 1983.

Hardt, Michael and Antonio Negri. *Empire*. Cambridge: Harvard University Press, 2000.

Hayes, Helene. *U.S. Immigration Policy and the Undocumented*. Westport: Praeger, 2001.

Hing, Bill. *To Be An American*. London and New York: New York University Press, 1997.

Huggan, Graham. *The Postcolonial Exotic: Marketing the Margins*. London and New York: Routledge, 2001.

Hune, Shirley. "Area Studies and Asian American Studies: Comparing Origins, Missions, and Frameworks." *Asian Americans: Comparative and Global Perspectives*. Eds. Shirley Hune, Hyung-chan Kim, Stephen Fugita, and Amy Ling. Pullman: Washington State University Press, 1991.

Huntley, E. D. *Amy Tan: A Critical Companion*. Westport, Connecticut & London: Greenwood Press, 1998.

Kim, Elaine H. *Asian American Literature: An Introduction to the Writings and Their Social Context*. Philadelphia: Temple University Press, 1982.

Kingston, Maxine Hong. *China Men*. New York: Vintage Books, 1980.

———. "Cultural Mis-readings by American Reviewers." *Asian and Western Writers in Dialogue: New Cultural Identities*. Ed. Guy Amirthanayagam. London: Macmillan, 1982.

———. *The Woman Warrior: Memoirs of A Girlhood Among Ghosts*, 1976. New York: Vintage, 1989.

———. *Tripmaster Monkey: His Fake Book*. New York: Vintage International, 1990.

Kitano, Harry. "Interview." *Roots: An Asian American Reader*. Ed. Amy Tachiki. Los Angeles: Continental Graphics, 1971.

Kwong, Peter. *The New Chinatown*. New York: Hill and Wang, 1987.

Lee, Robert. *Orientals: Asian Americans in Popular Culture*. Philadelphia: Temple University Press, 1999.

Li, David Leiwei. *Imagining The Nation: Asian American Literature and Cultural Consent*. Stanford: Stanford University Press, 1998.

Libretti, Tim. "America Is In The Heart." *A Resource Guide to Asian American Literature*. Eds. Sau-ling Cynthia Wong and Stephen Sumida. New York: The Modern Language Association of America, 2001.

Ling, Amy. "Chinese American Women Writers." *Maxine Hong Kingston's The Woman Warrior: A Casebook*. Ed. Sau-ling Cynthia Wong. New York and Oxford: Oxford University Press, 1999.

———. "The State of Asian American Studies in Wisconsin." *Reviewing Asian America*. Eds. Wendy Ng, Soo-Young Chin, James Moy, and Gary Okihiro. Pullman: Washington State University Press, 1995.

Liu, John and Lucie Cheng. "Pacific Rim Development and the Duality of Post-1965 Asian Immigration to the United States." *The New Asian Immigration in Los Angeles and Global Restructuring*. Eds. Paul Ong, Edna Bonacich, and Lucie Cheng. Philadelphia: Temple University Press, 1994.

Lowe, Lisa. *Immigrant Acts*. Durham and London: Duke University Press, 1996.

Ma, Sheng-Mei. *The Deathly Embrace: Orientalism and Asian American Identity*. London and Minneapolis: University of Minnesota Press, 2000.

McWilliams, Carey. *Brothers Under the Skin*. Boston: Little, Brown and Company, 1964.

McAlister, Melanie. "(Mis) Reading *The Joy Luck Club*." *Asian America: Journal of Culture and the Arts*. Winter 1992.

McLaren, Peter. "White Terror and Oppositional Agency: Towards a Critical Multiculturalism." *Multiculturalism*. Ed. David Theo Goldberg. Cambridge: Blackwell, 1994.

McWilliams, Carey. *Prejudice*. Boston: Little, Brown and Company, 1945.

Miyoshi, Masao. "Borderless World? From Colonialism to Transnationalism and the Decline of the Nation-State." *Critical Inquiry* 19 (1993): 726–51.

Mullings, Leith. "Ethnicity and Stratification in the Urban United States." *Racism and The Denial of Human Rights: Beyond Ethnicity*. Eds. Marvin Berlowitz and Ronald Edari. Minneapolis: MEP Publications, 1984.

Murashige, Michael. "Karen Tei Yamashita: Interview with Murashige." *Words Matter*. Ed. King-Kok Cheung. Honolulu: University of Hawaii Press, 2000.

Newfield, Christopher and Avery Gordon. "Multiculturalism's Unfinished Business." *Mapping Multiculturalism*. Eds. Avery Gordon and Christopher Newfield. London and Minneapolis: University of Minnesota Press, 1996.

Ng, Fae Myenne. *Bone*. New York: HarperPerennial, 1993.

Nguyen, Viet Thanh. *Race and Resistance*. New York and Oxford: Oxford University Press, 2002.

Okada, John. *No-No Boy*. Seattle: University of Washington Press, 1957.

Ozeki, Ruth. *My Year of Meats*. New York: Penguin Books, 1998.

Pozo, Mike Alexander. "An Educator's Reflections on the Crisis in Education and Democracy in the United States: An Interview with Henry A. Giroux." http://www.axisoflogic.com.

Rothenberg, Paula. "The Construction, Deconstruction, and Reconstruction of Difference." *Hypatia* 5 (1990): 46–49.

Sadowski-Smith, Claudia, Ed. *Globalization on the Line: Culture, Capital, and Citizenship at U.S. Borders*. New York: Palgrave, 2002.

———. "The U.S.-Mexico Borderlands Write Back: Cross-Cultural Transnationalism in Contemporary U.S. Women of Color Fiction." *Arizona Quarterly* 57 (2001): 91–112

San Juan, Edward. *On Becoming Filipino: Selected Writings of Carlos Bulosan*. Philadelphia: Temple University Press, 1995.

———. *Reading the West/Writing the East*. New York: Peter Lang, 1992.

Santa Cruz Collective on Labor Migration. "The Global Migration of Labor and Capital." *U. S. Capitalism in Crisis*. New York: URPE, 1978.

Sardar, Ziauddin. *Postmodernism and the Other*. London and Chicago: Pluto Press, 1998.

Schiller, Herbert. *National Sovereignty and International Communication*. Norwood: Ablex Publishers, 1979.

Schirmer, Danield and Stephen Rosskamm Schalom, Eds. *The Philippines Reader*. Boston: South End Press, 1987.

Shalom, Stephen Rosskamm. *The United States and the Philippines*. Philadelphia: A Publication of the Institute for the Study of Human Issues, 1981.

Spivak, Gayatri Chakravorty. "Can the Subaltern Speak?" *Marxism and the Interpretation of Culture*. Eds. Cary Nelson and Lawrence Grossberg. Urbana: University of Illinois Press, 1988.

Su, Karen. "Jade Snow Wong's Badge of Distinction in the 1990s." *Hitting Critical Mass: A Journal of Asian American Cultural Criticism* 2.1 (1994): 3–52.

Sweezy, Paul. *The Theory of Capitalist Development*. New York and London: Modern Reader Paperbacks, 1970.

Tachiki, Amy, Eddie Wong, Franklin Odo, and Buck Wong, Eds. "Success Story of One Minority Group in U.S." *U.S. News and World Report*. December 26, 1966. *Roots: An Asian American Reader*. California: The Regents of the University of California, 1971.

Takaki, Ronald. *Iron Cages*. New York: Alfred Knopf, 1979.

———. *Strangers From A Different Shore*. Boston, New York, and London: Little, Brown, 1989.

Tong, Benjamin. "Critic of Admirer Sees Dumb Racist." *The San Francisco Journal*. May 11, 1977.

Wallace, Molly. "Tropics of Globalization: Reading The New North America." *Symploke* 9 (2001): 145–60.

Wong, Jade Snow. *Fifth Chinese Daughter*, 1950. Seattle and London: University of Washington Press, 1989.

Wong, Morrison. "Post-1965 Asian Immigrants. " *The History and Immigration of Asian Americans*. Ed. Franklin Ng. New York and London: Garland Publishing Inc, 1998.

Wong, Sau-ling Cynthia. "Autobiography as Guided Chinatown Tour?" *Maxine Hong Kingston's The Woman Warrior: A Casebook*. Ed. Sau-ling Cynthia Wong. New York and Oxford: Oxford University Press, 1999.

———. *Reading Asian America Literature*. Princeton: Princeton University Press, 1993.

———. " 'Sugar Sisterhood': Situating the Amy Tan Phenomenon." *The Ethnic Canon*. Ed. David Palumbo-Liu. Minneapolis and London: University of Minnesota Press, 1995.

Yamashita, Karen Tei and Ryuta Imafuku. "The Latitude of the Fiction Writer: A Dialogue." http://www.cafecreole.net/archipelago/Karen-Dialogue.html.

Yin, Xiao-huang. *Chinese American Literature Since the 1850s*. Urbana and Chicago: University of Illinois Press, 2000.

Yung, Judy. *Unbound Voices: A Documentary History of Chinese Women In San Francisco*. London and Berkeley: University of California Press, 1999.

Index